The FootlooseBook

Marianna Kisvardai

Dedication

To my amazing Parents.

Contents

Do you Know or do you Understand?   15

Vision   29

   How do you find your vision?   30

Believe   45

Activities, networking and relations   57

   What is letitate?   67

   Do we have friends?   67

   You keep meeting the same spirits   75

   Distance relations   77

Accept yourself   93

   Giving away your spirit and mind   94

   Travelling alone   104

   Your type of work and company   116

Love and more   129

   No.Sex   144

Keep going, stay abroad   151

   Motivation   151

   Expectations   169

   The heavy stuff: Fear, hesitation, giving up   173

Just for fun   185

Bye for now and see you around   191

About the Author   195

Foreword

I am writing an amazing book.
It is not another I tell you what to do to be happy, to be famous and rich in 5 days and 10 steps book. Yet this will give you a list of solid foundations to start living with a new mindset and open to incredible opportunities. Those moments are everywhere and hanging low, there is no need to look for them or chase them. They are there and they are yours. Forever of a lifetime. Of course, always and only if you want to and when you go for it.

I'm writing this amazing book, it's not amazing because I said so. It is for its potential how much it can help you if you pick one or more of its tips and practicalities. I wish somebody would have shared such recommendations before I have started to travel the World, settled and lived in 11 different countries. You see, when it comes to travel and live abroad, lots of topics will come to discussion; such as how you should pack for your trip, what's the right luggage size, which items to where to carry, essentials for hand luggage if the sent one gets lost, how to ... but nobody would tell you how to handle the psychological aspects, the cultural differences, language barriers, environmental shocks, spiritual and the physical changes which will come along with your country moves. The emotional aspects of a relocation remain hidden. People want to seem strong and don't talk about this topic. These aspects look like weaknesses and we bury them inside when in reality, it's very important to work on them to be able to live healthily.

I do not wish to be famous. I only want to help. That's my dream. To contribute to people's happiness. Every dream come true was a plan first. So, let us consider this piece of writing as my concluded project towards that. And as this is my plot, I may describe it with any word. My word is amazing. I simply love the sound and the meaning of it. Most probably, I even fairly overuse it.

I am not a novelist or professional in writing, but I have been contemplating to throw my thoughts on paper for long years now. When I finally got started, the rush of inspiration suddenly vanished and my always chattering, creative Muse left my shoulders and would not whisper into my ears anymore. I was on hold. But I felt something different. Suddenly: calm! Soo calm like never before. I was set on my long-planned journey.
And this time, for the first time, it did not involve having a flight or train ticket.

I should not be alone with this statement: I just love the World and experience people. I have met thousands of people, listened to their stories, fairy tales, their own fables when they were up or down and savoured their experiences with them through their lens. I helped when I could, I smiled or cried when I should and enjoyed being part of the experience. Most of the time, it is not about the contribution but it's about fully listening and showing interest in others. I find it the most impressive how gender, cultural, religious or educational differences would not have any impact on how people feel and what they mostly struggle for. I am young, in fact I look very young as they say, but I was so lucky to travel the World and encounter many characters to learn from and with.

I quit my job. You finish on the top as my shooting coach (who happens to be my Dad)used to tell me...so it was my time, my peak, where I felt that I have learnt and experienced as much as I wanted in one industry. It was my time to move on and see the many wonders of the World. Life is too short to get stuck and stagnant and keep doing the same job, the same weekend activities, hobbies and dealing for the whole of it. That's a repetition of the same day for like 26280 days (a good 72 years lifespan).

I quit my job. Started writing.
Richard Branson said that everyone should write a book. A book of their life, a biography. I am not exactly writing a biography as who am I to write a biography with my age, especially. I want to share a lot though. Thanks to all the opportunities, I have spotted or created and took on in the past years, I can give you a few or more ideas how to live happily ever after and mainly, how to live everywhere.
Many friends have asked me what's your book about? What are you writing?
It's not a novel, not a biography and not the usual self-help book where you find explanations on daily struggles and a set of to-dos to tackle them. I simply want to share my experiences with you and along the stories will come my way and practises to deal with the moments when the sun won't shine on you and the light diminishes from the end of the tunnel. I had those moments. Plenty of them. I talk about those

moments to dispose them sort of. It doesn't make me a nagger and doesn't aim to drain anyone's energy around me. The opposite! It's registered on paper with the genuine goal to help.

Over the years, I have developed a "sense of soluting". I don't spend much time on the issue, but I see around for the tools and tricks to kill it quick and easy and mostly without a need of involving anyone else. You may call it any names; I did not build a whole theory around it or a www perfect trademark. I lived and live it. Every 86500 seconds of a day...now I'm lying...I sleep for a good 28800.

You will read a lot of my stories.

My book will not tell you anecdotes which you have never heard before, but it's mine and I promise you that you will have fun if you get into reading it.

When I write, I let people into my head. And that's a dangerous state. You can think you know what's going on up there, yet you would never see-feel-get exactly the same sensations and conclusions of what I have had.

Mind you, I'm not too smart on all the things of the big World. The corporate `businessness` sucked my acumen in and left me with no time or capacity to look outside and notice what's up in other fields. It is the only way to get on the top if you do all in and dedicate your flash and brain to one great thing. But I feel a lot. And feeling these days is dangerous. People can sense this and write it as a weakness on your side. I don't mind it. It's a pleasure most days and the other days when it hurts, I don't count them for a stone. I imagine life as some fairy-tale daydream which I can walk through with my eyes fixated on the sky and do good all the time and never get hurt. This is me, however part of the reality is that tough choices make good stories, so I went out for them. So far, I can say that life is not a cupcake with the sugar coating on the outside but a chocolate fondant with the rich sweet reward when you dig deep inside.

Curiosity is essential for progress. *"Only when we look to Worlds beyond our own can we really know if there is room for improvement"* (credit to Simon Sinek).
And keep in mind also, that just because you don't like something, it doesn't mean that it's wrong. Entertain the ideas before you send them for a home run forever.

Success tastes better when shared, for that reason, I recommend that you get a buddy who can hold your hand on the steep roads and keep your eyes on the summit. I suggest choosing someone you really trust, feel at ease to speak to and you can take some healthy criticism from.
It's also a crucial criterion to choose a person who is mutually interested in this exercise to become a better you, whatever better means to you at this stage of your life. Your buddy must deeply resonate with your current situation and where you want to be at the end of the adventure!
I did the same when writing this book! I chose a buddy to keep the push and pull, the everyday hassle, the moments when I feel, I would give up, to fill the gaps in my weaknesses and enrich me with his strengths. To make me a better me and to extend the brain capacity and the cumulative experiences in this

venture. We are the same type of crazy and made it through many practises and personal transitions, in different countries and cultural settings, to give you a great samples guide.

I have also given you a bite-sized summary at the end of each topic. I called it the Drip-Drops. I felt that you can use such just to turn back the pages and remind yourself on the milestones. Also, Albert Einstein said," *If you can't explain it simply, you don't understand it well enough"*, so there you go all concluded in few and plain points, ready served!

Lastly, this book is really a life act, produced by all who has appeared and crossed roads with me so far. It just happened that I gathered the thoughts on paper.
I must thank all my friends and by-passers who has thought me some or a lot and made me who I am today.
You see me as I am today however, there is no guarantee that I remain unchanged tomorrow.
Sort of like these ideas, suggestions, survival- tools; they are all fluid and they can be developed further or personalised.

Drip-Drops

You are reading `my amazing book` about all the unspoken aspects of travelling and relocating.

Enough for the prep.

Let's go!

Happy Footloose!

Do you Know or do you Understand?

I give you a vocabulary-like definition to start off with.

Knowledge: information gathering; knowledge is considered as power, so people are taking in all the data and info.

Understanding: having that knowledge and being able to apply it; how this knowledge conceptually is with different situations or people.

We all have at least a few theories or principles by which we should be living our lives. We gather that knowledge; we research the topics and we even discuss them with our friends or give them out as heartfelt advice. Commonly, we forget to put them in action and won't habituate them.

But are you actually using or practising them in your everyday or just embracing them on a nice idea level?
Is it because you do not spend enough time to study the topic, so you never get to its depths?
Are you changing your ideas too often?
Are you easily believing in fads and just follow them as hip talking topics, but you have no intention to seriously adapt them?
Are there a lot of vague concepts to tempt you but give no real remedy?
Are there too many influences coming to you in a short or same time?
Are you not content with what you are aiming for in your life, so the ideas won't work for you on a long run?
Is it then worth the time and energy to invest in

digging for deeper knowledge and eventual understanding of them?
Is there too much out there?
Are we overwhelmed with the information?
Are they served well-structured to pursue?
Are they practical or they only work on a theory level?
Do you really want to work them or them to work for you?

These are only a few questions running to my mind when thinking about knowing or understanding. And now let's look into this matter in more detail. In general, we can say that a good 85% of knowledge, we attain, will remain on the `cute fact we heard of` layer. We keep those conceptions and data on a shelf in the back of our mind. We remember of them in a given life situation. We even re-chant them and we feel the certainty that we are living by them. Then something happens, s**t hits the fan, to say bluntly, and we must face real life scenarios, we have previously heard and learned of, but we are not even close to be able to handle them.
We do know what we should do and how we should react! Right?
It cannot be that all those long hours, days spent on reading about life saving, crisis -crunching tactics, was all for nothing. We know the solution; we have the key to cross this door! But the door is not there, we don't find the lock and finally, the key is not fitting the lock ... our theory suffers and collapses right then and there.
Why does this happen? Simply because we forgot to

turn our knowledge into practical understanding.

I haven't finished University yet. In my 3rd year, I took on all the possible subjects to accumulate my credits and fill my 4th year ahead and decided to spend both of my last semesters on practical training. I always dreamed of the sunshine and loved to experience the sea - when we went to see it three times - so I decided to pick some exotic location. Through my high school IT teachers` suggestion, I connected to an old childhood friend and through her, posted my Trainee application to a dream resort in a sweet spot, called the Caribbean. At this time, I wouldn't have imagined, that they call me. Me? A girl from the most unknown European country; with a language which is only spoken here and not understood by anyone else in the Globe; worst, from a tiny city, not from the possibly recognised capital; and from an educational background which is highly rated on Hungarian scale but not exactly as famous as Cambridge. I had given it 0.001% chance that they would pick me. Yet, one day my phone rang. I had that super Nokia 5110 brick phone and was very proud of it. A wonderful voice with incredibly sweet Jamaican accent – I had no idea at this time, that it was Jamaican accent of course, but got 0 of 5 words of what she said- had ask me if I am still interested to join their resort as a Trainee. Do not ask me how but I made it through this luckily short phone screening interview and the next rounds were just tons of written arrangements. In the following weeks, I spent my days with the preparation for my Traineeship. I applied for the J1D visa, interviewed at the US Embassy and pertained all the documentation necessary. In the meantime, I started to discover St Thomas, my destination and home for the coming 18 months. I have read a travel book, that was all I could find. Ok, seven pages of a travel book about the Caribbean Islands, to be precise, as this was all available on the market. Wherever I went and whoever, I have turned to, had no clue what I meant when I confidently said that I need information about St Thomas in the US Virgin Islands. I gathered a few more crumbs from online, obviously, back then, the internet had no vast information on the topics, yet I managed to see a few photos, mainly of hotel websites. The excitement when looking at those photos on the internet, overwrote everything and I had no suspicion what's coming at me.

I have packed my life in a 25kg luggage and took off on my second in my lifetime flight, heading to a tiny Caribbean island, St Thomas. If I only understood what I was doing, I would have been in cold sweat from fear and my heart would have left my chest from pumping too hard. Luckily, I only knew what move I have made. I set my sail towards a spot which, I could not even locate in the World Atlas...I had to search online to find where exactly it was. How crazy that sounds? Isn't it? With 22, you think that you can change the World, and anything is possible - I got stuck at that age-mentality by the way - so I packed things which I imagined they can come handy in the Caribbean. In a place where I have never been to, nor anyone of my relatives or friends; where I knew nobody and had no idea what or whom waits for me. The plane took off. There was no turning back. No Skype, no Whatsapp....only a 3kg dinosaur laptop with the MSN messenger program, a portable camera, a plugin headset for the microphone and a slight hope that once a week, I get reception to call someone, I clearly and entirely understand. Admittedly, not understanding often saves us from not trying. That I consider as a great benefit of the whole knowing to understanding process.

My flight had landed in Miami and I was informed that a taxi driver with my name on a sign will pick me up and take me to a sister hotel of ours. I had to spend an overnight here to catch my connection on the next morning. From Komárom to Miami. Back than my German was much more fluent than my English and suddenly I found myself in the backseat of a taxi, cruising Oceans Drive and talking to the old guy about what to do and what to see in the city in just one day. He had offered me a tour and as I felt he was genuine, just agreed to it. In that instance, I even call myself lucky that I had zero knowledge of what could happen with taxi drivers. I probably never used a taxi before, so I was just going by my gut feeling and my mind was not pre-filled with any of the possible horror stories. We agreed to meet up in one hour, it gave me time to check-in, shower and dress for the beachy climate. Here it is my time to confess that apart from this trip being my second flight ever, fourth visit to the seaside, it happened to be my first time checking into a hotel. And back then, I really kept count of all these significant events. They were rare like a white crow -as our old saying goes. I have travelled a lot in my young years and I consider myself lucky that I could have visited most of Europe due to the efforts of my parents and the sport I have practised, but we have stayed in student accommodation, slept on the floors of sports halls or shooting ranges or did some fun camping. Approaching the reception and being told that they have been expecting me and the General Manager of the other hotel had reserved me a wonderful room, kept me breathless for minutes. Right before I would have fainted, the porter approached me to help with my luggage. It was slightly disturbing how much attention they have given to me and that not only the luggage guy had escorted me to the room but also the hotel manager came along. After a quick shower, I was ready to discover the city. The hours past fast and the driver was really kind, he had given me some time to walk on Oceans Drive and then picked me up as promised so I could return safe and sound to my hotel and get a good night sleep. I took some photos with my then upgraded Nokia 8110, hoping that one day, I can share them with my loved ones. It was all so surreal; I had no time to even register what was happening. It all felt as walking in a daydream. I was a blank page, had no idea of this part of the trip, not prepared what to expect in Miami and the bit where at least I had some knowledge of, was just coming as next.

All in all, it was such a memorable first hotel stay. The next flight had landed in St Thomas. Let me first explain to you how this descend looked like. The plane was dipping and diving, they have prompted us to fasten the seatbelt for the landing. The aircraft was rapidly nearing the ocean, but no land could have been seen. Not far, not near. Naturally, I took a window seat to monitor all the happenings and in general, I love the sight of the clouds and the lights playing on the top of the sky. We were getting closer and closer and I started to question if this was a normal landing manoeuvre or the pilot had mistaken the airstrip by few miles. There was nothing under us. I could suddenly see the reflection of the plane in the ocean and in a second, we were about to touch water. Closed my eyes and took a deep breath, possibly I also said how much I love my family and a short mental bye to them. When the plane bounced back from the tarmac. The bloody airstrip was just a slim stretch built on the sea. It was invisible from above and even when nearing it. I was wowed.

It was the start of something, I never knew would happen to me. A long time, if not a lifetime love, a deep obsession with the tropics, a music of your heartbeat, which a drum cannot beat, which you only feel when the plane door opens, and the salty sweet rotten fruity and flowery humid scent brushes your nose. It goes deep, into my veins. Not only into my lungs. It's my happy drug and the only one I am taking and want to stay an addict to it. It's euphoria. I have collected my luggage and stepped into the arrival hall. There was no indication who is going to pick me up at the airport, so I just waited to see if I notice a sign with my name again. I did not spend a full minute staring at this new site, a tall gentleman in a suite had approached me, took my luggage and started walking with long strikes. He probably had introduced himself and said something else however I could not catch a single word of what he said. I knew English but I didn't understand. Not only because of the strong dialect, he was using. Speaking a language involves the same principle as any theoretical knowledge. It must be applied before you can fully put it in use. All the accumulated learning would not work for you without long hours, days and

21

years of practise to lead you to full understanding. Back to the scene, well, I had no choice but to trust this extremely tall and masculine stranger. He had a warm smile. It, kind of, kept me calm. He took me to his pickup jeep, throw my bag at the back and opened the door for me. At this point, he must have read it from my face how not convinced I was, so he smiled and said: -Donworry, I`m gud friend to the GM of the hotel. He couldn` come, asked me to drive you to the resort. His talk was somewhat clearer, and I understood these two sentences at least. We drove through wonderful paths, crazy zig-zagging roads with lush tropical forests and oceanside. Shores which can't be described or pictured but must be seen and felt. I still had no idea what I was doing and naturally did not even registered where I was. My travel companion was trying to hold up a conversation, he was extremely light-hearted and polite. Also, he realised that I was not familiar with his West-Indies accent, so he struggled his fair share to promptly articulate the words. During the 30 minutes or so drive, we managed to get on well and even put up a small chat. He turned into and parked at the lower reception of the resort and kindly bid farewell.

Upon arriving to the hotel, there was one of my future colleagues collecting me, his name was Morris. I have never met with such a warm, carefree and natural person. He hugged me and welcomed me to the family. I was shocked. In Europe, you would never receive a genuine hug from a stranger and probably one would never welcome you in the family on your new job. Morris was driving a mid-size, four-wheel drive, convertible, SUV, turbo, pearl-white with leather seats, golf cart. That two minutes slope leading up to the main reception, he really made it a sporty ride. He continued talking, telling stories about the island and the hotel. His mood and voice were totally uplifting, I have enjoyed it so much even if it sounded as a new language, I have never heard before. I got to know more of him in these two minutes than what you would figure out about your thirty years long office neighbour in any desk job back at home. This is not a conclusion based on my own experience, of course.

The fun ride was followed by my second check in and I was assigned my new home for the coming one and a half years. It was a beautiful and spacious room with a huge bathroom but mainly what I have noticed was a long balcony with unobstructed views of the Caribbean Sea. And palm trees, plenty of them. And sunshine, striking, hot and humid. I must have fainted on that balcony standing there with this sight. Only got back to life when noticed the voice of my roommate who had approached me and then she got closer and tapped on my shoulders. We have introduced to each other. She was also a Trainee, already there for few months. After some talking, she offered to show me around the resort and made me acquainted with the other Trainees.

I felt enormous happiness but by then, I finally knew that I understood nothing of this new adventure.

This was just a small snap of my first quest. I could go on to show you and explain how amplified all the experiences felt and how radically different my new environment was. I was not prepared even when confidently thinking that I knew what I was going for.

Neither having the knowledge nor feeling mentally ready could replace the real-life drill. Understanding and by that having the certainty comes only through action. No theory can replace that.

I will repeat myself here to stand tall for the travellers, expats and adventure seekers. Admittedly, not understanding often saves us from not trying. That I consider as a great benefit of the whole knowing to understanding process.

Finding the difference between knowing and understanding can be challenging. It is hard to find a distinction between the two because they are both abstract processes of the mind and the brain. Being able to know their differences can lead us to a better awareness of ourselves, who we are, and what we want.

Knowing, or the act of knowing, which is called knowledge, is defined as a skill acquired by an individual through learning. It includes facts and information and involves the basic recall of ideas which have been previously presented. We believe that having access to more information produces more knowledge, which results in more wisdom. But, if anything, the opposite is true - more and more information without the proper context and interpretation only muddles our understanding of the World rather than enriching it. Knowledge involves perception, learning, communication, association, and reasoning. It may also mean the ability to use a certain thing or subject for an appropriate purpose. All information is processed and then related to a person, object, situation, or messages which require an individual to think and use concepts to deal with.

24

Also called intellection, understanding involves conceptualization and association. It is the awareness of the connection between pieces of information that are presented and has a deeper level than knowing and, in fact, is essential in order to put knowledge to good use. For example, you may also recognize a written language and know what it is just by looking at the characters, but you will not understand it unless you take time to study it. Understanding instead of knowing is just a different approach. Pursuing a life of understanding rather than trying to be right needs a lot of energy because it requires consistent change not only of your views but your mind. Change is uncomfortable, and just because it's consistent doesn't mean it gets easier. In order for the brain to understand, it must be presented with the same knowledge constantly. The more practical information that the brain receives about a subject, the better it will understand, that's why it's recommended to read, see and hear something in order to learn it best. When you understand, you can distinguish, explain, interpret, and summarize data. When you know, you are able to identify, label, list, name, and recall the information. Both understanding and knowing are very important for our growth as individuals. They determine how we view and react to our environment and the people we associate with.

Vietnamese Buddhist monk Thich Nhat Hanh offers his perspective on what it means to truly understand something: *"Penetration means to enter something, not just to stand outside of it. When we want to understand something, we cannot just stand* *outside and observe it. We have to enter deeply into it and be one with it in order to really understand. If we want to understand a person, we have to feel their feelings, suffer their sufferings, and enjoy their joy. The sutra uses the word `penetration` to mean `full comprehension. `The word `comprehend` is made up of the Latin roots; com, which means `together in mind, `and `prehendere`, which means `to grasp it or pick it up `. So, to comprehend something means to pick it up and be one with it. There is no other way to understand something."*

I really liked his definition and agree that you must start to get involved in situations rather than just observe them from the outside and by that, you will be able to enter a deeper level of understanding. You can learn, read, investigate, and apply until you get to understand the matter, and I have to tell you that all the learning is a good thing, but the real secret to success is in the application. That combination of knowledge and application is all you really need to succeed and that may sound grossly simplified, but that really is the way it is. And according to my humble experiences, from knowing to understanding is a long way, just because you have tried to take action, this will not make you an expert and will not make the practised skill or habit, part of you.

You can play a tiny exercise! Such an easy example will get you convinced on the `knowledge applied in practise is a must to reach understanding` idea.
Please just give it a try!
Open Google and search for a riddle. Pick the first one.
Take the cues - read it.

See the description and the solution - interpret it.
Now you know this riddle!
Action - prepare to tell the same riddle to your friends.
Do - perform the action and discuss their conclusions with them.
How does it feel after the discussion?
You will say that the riddle looks easy now as you understand it though your practise!

Why would I have rolled up all this sweet theory about such a simple concept and what is the reason for a lengthy discussion of the knowing-understanding topic when this was supposed to be a book about travelling and relocation?
Do you know the quote from Confucius *"Every journey starts with one first step"*? Beautiful. This hints exactly where I was heading to, to say that until you make your first move, you can be extremely well prepared and knowledgeable however without the starting step, you will not understand what taking a journey means.
I wanted you to be mentally ready for the first hits and be prepared exactly not to understand!

Drip-Drops

Knowledge can be gathered by learning.

You get to understand things through practical actions.

You can know billion things but ideally, you understand the things that are practical to you in your everyday life.

Admittedly, not understanding often saves us from not trying. That I consider as a great benefit of the whole knowing to understanding process.

Vision

Big word, nobody knows what it is! lol!
So, let me be the smart egg who guides you on this or at least in the bush...for now!
Let's start with few questions:
1.) Describe in one sentence, what you are doing right now?
2.) Explain in short, what you will be doing in 1-year time?
3.) What are the 3 most significant differences between now and then?
4.) Which steps you will take to get there?
Okay, if you have answered the first question, that's a great base to build on. It shows that you are clear on your current situation and you have foundational ideas of your starting point.
If you have answered the second question, that means that you have some goals in front of you.
You got the first two but struggle on the third one? It feels somehow certain, but the steps are not crystal clear yet. You came to the right place to form and firm your vision! As you are reading this book you can get ideas on how to get there...!
Got to answer number 4 too? Gal, Man, you are rollin`. You have a vision in fact and a solid one! You are set; flip the book through, share your how-to-dos with the others on our www.thefootloosebook.com website and keep going!

You stayed with me, so I assume that not all the answers were evident. You have some ideas, I am certain, but we need to have a sharper focus and funnel your energies into the right direction.

`I don't know what I want...` the most searched expression on Google. Believe it or not. You do not know what to do, what you want and who you want to become. There is no simple solution to this. Vision helps you to make better decisions, move into your desired direction, keeps you on the path and to constantly aim at your goal, and to stay content in and with any circumstances. Because you know why you have chosen to be where you are, to do what you do; periodically, you can clearly evaluate if the situation is taking you from your point A to B. Or from and to any point you wish to be moving between; or if you just want to grow at point A, then your vision will always be your lighthouse to guide you to your best in that moment.

How do you find your vision?

Firstly, you could go and ask your family or friends. I often relied on them to advise me in my milestones. I heard flattery comments about my capabilities and accomplishments and great pointers what I must do with such skills and capacities. I went exact zero distance with those nice words. As generic human behaviour suggests, you wouldn't fully believe what others say about you, as your self-opinion is kicking you stronger in most cases. Here is a quick proof; when your coach tells you after the game that you have done great, but you feel your performance was s**t, which impression is stronger? Which one you will take home? Which one leaves an imprint and will pop up during the next training or game?
So, asking for advice to get your vision instantly, is

useless, in fact.

Secondly, you can try out things and pursue various paths. I became overly enthusiastic and started to race a marathon with a sprint speed. I wanted to do more and more, having an agenda of a high-level executive, a gardener at my home, a kindergarten nanny to my sister, a cabaret dancer when out with friends, an orchestra player and a future Olympic champion. (I was a hotelier...well it is more or less the same as all the previous together.)

Shortly after I have moved from London to Malta-throw the sunseeker move-, I was approached by a local guy via social media. Normally, I would not start a chat with a stranger on such platforms, but his way felt genuine. And he started by praising my father for his coaching and his athletes` achievements. So, I heard him out. He was inviting me to join their shooting team and if I liked it, start competing with them. After few weeks, we finally managed to get to the range. They have geared me up with some old clothing which hanged on me rather than fitted, and a rifle, which, I probably would only use if that was the last option of all. At that point, it was not so important; I was holding a rifle again and could enjoy few hours to practise my beloved but long not trained sport. I was on the roll and kept scoring nicely centred 10s. I guess about an hour could have passed. When I have turned back to say something to my new buddy, I noticed that half of the club stood behind and stared at me. They appreciated what they saw. There was no doubt, that I should join them and start representing Malta with the shooting team. I was happy and excited. The only questionable factor was time. Beside my 12-14 hours on 6 days job, gym to keep me sane, practising music, keeping in touch with my family and friends abroad and some squeezed social time in my new home country, there was not much left, unless, I would have tried not to sleep at all. Still, I wanted it so badly, I went for it. I was on the Maltese National Shooting Team and participated many great competitions, training camps and had ample of fun with this amazing bunch of athletes. I have won few medals too. We participated at Small Nations Games, Commonwealth Games and some international derbies, mainly in Italy. It was a great honour when Malta voted me to be one of their Sportswoman of the year. I was flattered to be invited for the fascinating gala and some local TV shows. I got my dream back to pursue the Olympics. I could feel that I belonged to a fine group where likeminded people shared the spirit of sport. We have supported each other and learned from each other. It was both uplifting and exhausting. I kept going at the Lamborghini-speed to keep up with all my commitments. I cut out time from resting, saying to myself that training is my rest and competing is my way to relax and when travelling for the games or camps, I addressed those times as holidays.

You can close your eyes for a second and meditate on this picture. Looks glamorous, doesn't it? I managed to divide my resources and spread them all over so much, that at the end I did nothing but exhausted myself. My energy drained and won't get me to the end goal.

It's not with regret how I look back to this time, more as one of the best periods in my life. I am grateful to live through such an intense course as all this exposure, bonds and action brought me closer to see that doing everything is practically doing nothing. For every chapter in life, we shall have one main focus and stream our energy to build upon it. If you give a small raindrop everywhere, it won't fill the pool for you to swim, you must collect all the drops in the same basin if you want to stay afloat.

Thirdly, what's left? You must ask yourself. You need to search within, to know what your lookout in your life is, your perspective, your values and those will all help you to find your future cast.
Here is a way to find your forte, interest and build your vision for your amazing life!
Keep a list on your bedside table, on the fridge or someplace where you can always see it.
You must write at least one note into each category, every single day.

You can tear out the page on the right with your exercise notes.

Mark down these points:

What I enjoyed the most:
(- passions)

What made me feel good / happy / proud:
(-strengths= you do it as a flow / low effort for a high and easy success)

What I want more of:
(-interests / desires)

Focus on today! There is only today, no yesterday and no tomorrow!
After one month, see the most repeated expressions. There you go, that's where your focus should be. If you carry on for longer, you funnel down your real angle and get to your crystal-clear outlook, as sharp as a Japanese katana!

There is another great way to get to the end goal. This let's call it, a method, is exactly playing on your struggles. When you don't know what you want, it is easier to know what you don't want, what you don't like or even what is not working already. Take note of them! We will use them just in a minute. That's your starting point to lead you to your desires.

Let's cook it a little more! Take a pinch of your dreams too. At the beginning, dreams are too fragile to capture and to lead you to detailed plans. Instead of chasing a ready-in-a-minute solution; incubate. Work on other things, play, discuss with as many people as you can, get insights. Then research, study, immerse yourself in the many versatile and potential ways. Play with the hows and what ifs until you have digested all the floating thoughts and you have seared the most valuable ones for you to take them to the making. All you need is imagination while at this play (and plenty of patience, curiosity and empathy too).
In the making, the purpose is progress, not perfection! You will be launching version 1.0. And now, keep adding on, keep fine-tuning. Scan for what you like on the draft and amplify it! Do not have the final goal in mind such as by 3.0 this `product` must

be a Six Sigma and finished to an end. Such doesn't exist and won't happen. It is not a machine generated algorithm, you are searching for, it is your life-vision! What you have thought of at the first steps of the journey, now has been converted into a more working and in-the-make group of ideas. It's been shaped and paved by influences, partners, friends, and pushed under the press to see if it withstands the test called real life. Your initial idea has been shuffled by at least 50% and must keep being adapted. The chances are significantly higher that this progress would not stop. Unless you stop and give up the creative transformation towards your vision.

While swimming upstream, it may feels alone at times. Look for means to indulge in this creation. Do what make you be well, go to the beach, watch the sunset, do crosswords, learn knitting. Your social life won't fill the gap between your old life without a vision and the new still-in-the-brew life where you are heading to. At times when thinking and experimenting feels overwhelming and you lose sight of the goal, breathe! Find better ways and different ways to interact with the World and continue with the transition. Excitement must fuel you! Adrenalin will burn in you and crave pushes you forward. It is a wonderful ride! Enjoy!

Orna Ross, indie publisher and psychologist said; *"Once you grasp what you want, it is a mistake to pin it like a butterfly to the wall. Let the intention float around you. Let it settle."*

I found myself in the crossroads many times, when two souls, inner ideas were fighting. I used the same mental exercises noting down my wants and don't wants, asking around but not settling with any suggestions rather use them as new inputs to trigger my own thinking and debates and an enormous amount of patience to figure out what will be my next move and how I need to work on myself.

In my second year, working in Malta, I was approached with a nice opportunity. The hotel manager proposed a task force position for me to relocate to Cyprus and restructure the front teams, appoint and train new leadership for them. It came very unexpected. I was at a stage where I felt settled on the island, I had my home, were succeeding in my job, had great hobbies and built strong support from a circle of good friends. My intention was more to develop in this setting rather than start anew somewhere else.

Back in my younger days, I would have never imagined that I will travel from country to country and live everywhere. I was a very devoted kid to my parents and could not even do a sleep over at my grandparents who live 5 miles away from our place. My grandparents had few midnight-runs when they rolled me home on the bicycle. I bless them for their care and love, for saving me from a sleepless night and naturally saving themselves from listening to a few hours of my crying.

For some miraculous mind and heart-change and mainly for the distraction of the wonderful people and places, I was lucky to savour; I was now about to move to country number five. My boss showed me his full trust when he came up with this offer. And believe me, he was a tough one to please, with strict frames and short loops. It meant a lot to me to be considered for such a proposition. Few days were spent in contemplating. I have written a full inventory of pros and cons, consulted my insiders to gather some more remarks and sat on the edge of Dingli cliffs – which is my secret spot when I need to immerse in my thoughts and feelings – to see which way I can best pursue my vision. I stood on the line to pick: do I stay settled and grow slow or keep moving and develop diverse? I presume, you know which I have selected...

"Sometimes we need to lose our way to find our way!" as Robin Sharma says. So, I did and keep doing. It takes self-discipline to observe your life in such an analytical manner and it feels like a lab-rat at times. But just when you would run out of thoughts, then will come the best ideas. Your dreams are closer than you think!

I urge you to find a direction and start today! It doesn't matter how far you want to go; you always need to take just one step.

Yes, however the question is, if you are heading into the right direction? Before you start walking till you sweat and you resist on your run, you might make sure that you are facing the desired summit. Check day by day, take measures and build your confidence from the daily accomplishments. The small achievements will lead you to find your strengths. You have those strengths to build your life around them and to fulfil your everyday when practising them. You become the person who you oat to be and find support and evidence from all sorts of sources when you know what to look out for. The more you experiment the closer you get to a nicely shaped vision.

Why to have a vision? I mean what's living with a vision or having goals and purpose for your life? If you don't know where you are going, any road will take you there...but you are not getting anywhere.

I heard an interesting idea once: that life is made up by units- units according to the activity's length. Breakfast, lunch and dinner are one unit, grocery shopping one unit, gym 2 units, walk to work one unit, walk home one unit, cooking one unit, cleaning one unit, reading two units...This made me think , how you can build up the day like a Tetris game and make your life seam full with trivially measured activities. You can interpret the fullness as fulfilled when in fact, it is just full. If it doesn't mean anything, it is not heading you anywhere.

Ask anyone who has ever achieved anything, they must tell you, that all they have started with, was first just a vision, an idea. That's like a seed. Then they contemplated on it, spent time figuring the depths, shaping few pointers, concrete goals out of it. Like roots. After came the experimenting, seeing few directions to head towards. Like the small branches springing out of the soil. The strongest ones survive, those became the trunk of the tree. And spring comes with all the leaf and flowers when your ideas have grown into a flourishing vision with all the aspects worked out and with a strong foundation made up out of your values, dreams and experiences. Only if we have a vision, it can take us to personal fulfilment! You feel accomplished and in balance when you find and follow your call.

Today authenticity is your highest currency.

I have an interesting exercise to find the vision of your true self. It is from the great Mr Warren Buffett, whom I cherish not for his fortune but for his brilliant and humble humanity.
Grab a piece of paper and a pen.
Draw a straight vertical line in the middle of the sheet.
Think of somebody whom you want to be or would like to change places with them.
List what you admire in them on the left side of the paper. You find those in yourself too!
Now think of a person whom you don't bear and list what you can't stand them, on the right side of the paper. You find these qualities in yourself too!
You can do the same in a different mind-play. Think of your `Fairy godmothers or godfathers`, role models whose behaviour, attitude and strengths they have represented, their significance in your life you want to copy and follow and use it as an inspiration and relate to?!
Then find their opposite, the impact on people you surely do not want to have, their approach which tickles you and puts you off with a zero-tolerance limit.
Behaviour becomes a habit, so if you keep doing the things on the left side of your list, then in a while, you find that you are the person you most admire. Which will allow you to drive your life towards your vision of yourself.

Embrace the chaos at the beginning, live the guesswork in the making and have fun when you already start figuring out your ways!

Drip-Drops

Vision helps you to make better decisions, move into your desired direction, keeps you on the path and helps you to stay content in and with any circumstances.

For every chapter in life, we shall have a main focus and stream our energy to build upon it.

Whatever you are doing, it's worth overdoing it!
Daymond John – The People`s Shark

In the making, the purpose is progress, not perfection! Scan for what you like on the draft and amplify it!

Believe

This chapter could have been just a subdivision within Vision as they go well together. Fairly, they only go side by side. However, I felt that I must emphasise the importance of it and made it a full flesh short but meaningful independent episode.

When you are somewhere far from home alone and a huge decision is due to be made. What is the best way to handle it?
Your beloved family and friends would have no idea of the environment you are living in, they do not know the sites, the surroundings, the culture, the society, the life and work pace, the expectations, the language, your new community. How would they be able to support you in your decisions? You will surely paint a reasonably detailed picture and hear them out, to comfort yourself. Their suggestions can hardly push your choice in any direction as their opinions are based on their life experiences and environments which can be greatly working for them, though not convincingly where you are.
Your new folks are surely great connections however you need digestion time to build strong bonds which makes it difficult to trust your life-decisions on their advice. Undoubtedly, you share a few pointers of your situation and consult them as the local experts. Still, your gut feeling won't let you settle with their suggestions.
What is there to turn to?
Your vision and your own beliefs.
That is your solid foundation which helps your clear judgement. Which makes you totally unshakable in

any given life situation, location or time-zone. It enables you to decide even when alone and to feel certain with your choices.

Believe.

I am not talking about any particular religion. I am not talking about religion at all. Believe in something that keeps you on the go, believe firm and solid. Keep believing and keep going until it makes you push harder, aim further and jump higher. When you tired yourself out and there is no dust of adrenalin around, then it is time to find a new belief. Some will be churchgoers, some will be sun-followers, some will worship stones or objects, and few will believe in an idol or mystique. And the least of you will believe in yourselves.

All of them sound equally incredible.

The ultimate goal would be that you have an indescribable, strong pull towards an ideology or set of systems and you build it on a base of believing in yourself. You must know that you are capable to execute anything you have planned up and practised for long enough. Call me naive, crazy or a dreamer. However, I really do believe that anything is possible. You only must set your mind to it and then you find a way to make things happen. Same in finding beliefs. You must make sure that your belief system gives you cushioning and the drive, so when you arrive to rough roads, you will be able to turn your face up and walk as if it was just a morning stroll in the park. No excuses, no changing of your mind and no freakin' way not to feel good and not to live happily ever after.

How do I find my beliefs?
Do I choose them, or they come to me?
Do I manifest them?
How do they show up when they are needed?
How do I know if it is the right thing for me to follow?
How can I make my beliefs strong and part of me and my every day?
When is it enough? Ever?
Do I need to change my beliefs? Can I live a lifetime with the same set of thoughts and ideas?

When we move or our life circumstances are changing, we make a mistake to still search for the same usual things. We need to let go of the old habits and build new routines. You change, your life situation changes, you read and hear new things, make new friends and acquaintances. All these turbulences are serving you their delights and might lead you to a new and shinier yellow brick road. Make your vision and beliefs fit into the new setting and dare to shape them as you feel it is needed. Just remember that Alice had to fall to get to Wonderland!

Intuition is one way to lead yourself to your beliefs. It is not a rare commodity of monks. You can use it and you don't even need to sit around and wait for it. There are well thought, scientific methods to trigger your intuition (Read about it on www.mindvalley.com). You can tap into that deep reservoir and make use of this source for your benefit. It is a great tool, especially when you are in a new place and it's hard to trust the new people around or there is nobody to turn to for advice. Not only in these extreme scenarios but I truly believe that intuition serves us well in any given situation.

Reading gives you many impressions. I always loved to turn the pages of life-stories, biographies, self-help and science books or magazines on various subjects and highlight a few sentences which resonated with me the most. The ideas gathered, blended with my own thoughts, I have shaped them into practical and boosting daily routines. These readings and at times listening to podcasts or YouTube talks has guided me to form my beliefs and strengthen the feeling of knowing and trusting myself.

We don't need to go far to find examples on how we learn, accept and apply some common beliefs. National traditions are fundamental concepts which grew into us and we now practise them with no doubt. They become part of our days and years, so they turn to be part of us. I will not describe widely celebrated holidays but wish to introduce you to one of my personal favourites. Baba Marta from Bulgaria. She is a mythical figure who brings the end of the cold winter and the beginning of the spring. She is celebrated in Bulgaria on the first of March with the exchange and wearing of martenichki. The tradition of giving friends red-and-white interwoven strings brings health and happiness during the year and is a reminder that spring is near. One will wear the martenichki until finds the first blooming fruit tree or a stork bird. Then you will need to tie your bracelet on the tree or place it under a rock and based on what you find there the next morning, guesses what kind of a year this one will be. Two of my best friends are originally from Bulgaria, I have met them while living in Malta and was given these bracelets year by year. Now that we are not in the same country, they would even post the wrist-pieces to me or we purposely plan a meet-up for the beginning of March.

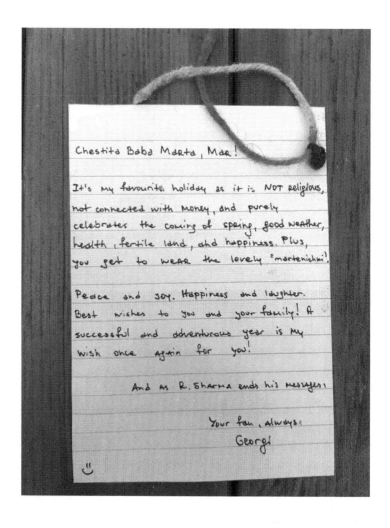

During my period in the Seychelles, I have discovered a very cute and beautiful place. I took my usual ride to clear my head after a hectic week or two and ended up on a hilltop with a spectacular view. I entered this charming blue and white house without a running thought that this could be someone's private house. A hacienda-like layout welcomed me. The arches were much shorter and simpler than usually, but the inner courtyard was lavishly full of colourful tropical flowers. The scene and the scents, I was smelling, were making me feel as if I was on a new island. Somewhere far away from anything I have ever known. I passed through the garden and entered the cute reception room which looked like a restaurant. The view from here opened and I could now see the whole West side of Mahe, (the main island in the Seychelles) with all the other near islets. A lady had approached me from behind. I probably passed her desk, as I was very focused on and fascinated by the place. She kindly asked how she could help me. Later, she has explained that this is a small retreat where they have a holistic approach to bring their guest to a balanced state or heal them. They offer treatments, reiki, yoga and, they produce their own all natural and mostly home-grown remedies. I did not have an idea of the place, yet, felt instantly relieved and just wanted to stay more to enjoy the energy of this magnetic and deeply tranquil spot. On that day, I took a massage and kept returning for one every now and then. I also have used their beauty products and essential oils to cheat and bring the silence of Sans Souci into my chaotic days.

Two and a half years later, I have returned to the

island. One of my first trips has led me to this special place. I was with my friend and we wanted to enjoy a treatment, but they were fully booked, so we decided to check out the shop for one or few remedies. When we have approached the counter to question the lady there, I had a very strong and sudden feeling as if I had known her for a while and I knew who she was. I just addressed her and said you must be the owner of this place- she smiled and answered with a yes. We carried on with a long conversation about how she has established this place where harmony is created while nature is preserved. All I felt is that I have arrived. It was a connected and quiet impression. I could feel her words and I sensed that she really believed in the healing power of this spot and the incredibly strong energies of the surrounding nature. For her, I also believed and `felt the calming breeze unwinding me, out of the clutters of the mind and into this moment`.

When someone has a firm take on their life approach and they live out their values, they become so infectious that it's nearly impossible to resist. Especially if you already carry similar value-sets. You will easily enter their bubble and find yourself on the same wavelength. It is beautiful to see how the owner`s faith had transformed not only the site but all those who has ever passed this enchanting place. [1]

Experience showed that there is no pattern, rule, frame, time, restriction when it comes to our beliefs. As long as you stay well and you do not offend anyone around you, you may practise anytime and

---

[1] www.thestationseychelles.com

any ceremonies, rituals, mantras, songs, prayers or chanting. You do not live for the outside; this is all about you. It is a working power to make you the best of yourself. No need to stick it on the billboard. Your morning ritual is not a cafeteria topic with your workmates, - hopefully - either your beliefs should be. When people don't know you so well, it can come out funny if you tell them how you rub your stones and chant your songs to boost your energies in your home or for an important meeting. You can share with your inner circle where you are accepted. Not necessarily understood but accepted, which is the highest level of resonance, what we should demand from our close persons, and never more.

I had long conversations when a friend or two made a strong attempt to run me for a change and do what they do to steel their spirits. It made me suffocate and I could never assimilate with the foreign ideas when they were served on a lavish plate, but unfortunately after a big dinner...I had no space and no need for them in my life at that moment, I was satisfied and even if not, I did not appreciate the crest they brought over me to try to suck me into their ocean. You will not become better in your life by pushing your views on someone or trying to copy-paste their ideas into your belief-system. No one will benefit from it unless it is their free choice to go along and start practicing the same or something else to better their life and circumstances.

You may pick and choose one or a hundred times; you need to make it deep-rooted and really internalise it. And make it work. No other terms or conditions apply.

Don't let people scare you off from your destiny, you can't go through life, trying to please everyone. The person, you must please, is the one who looks at you in the mirror. Worry not about what others will think of you and let go of any judgements on others. Live your life, no one will live it for you!

Before I get you to our concluding lines, I want to show you how we work with our beliefs and motives. Do you read astrology?

If you do, then just follow me, if not, please read your 2019 predictions and then come back here.

Professor Bertram Forer asked his students to fill in a personality test, based mainly on their birth dates, times and such. Then, he handed out the exact same result to each one of them. After the test, he has asked them to rate if the analysis was accurate on a 1-5 scale if this really described their personality traits. The majority rated the accuracy of the outcomes at 4! This was the prediction which they all have received:

`You very much need others to appreciate you and to esteem you, yet you have a tendency to be critical of yourself. Despite having some weaknesses in the character, you are generally able to remedy it. You have many unused skills that you have not turned to your advantage. Disciplined and controlled on the outside, you tend to be worried and insecure within you. Sometimes you seriously doubt that you have made the right decision or have done the right thing. You prefer a certain amount of change and variety and you feel dissatisfied if bound to restrictions and limitations. You pride yourself on being independent in your ideas and not accepting the opinions of others

without a test that satisfies you. But you have discovered that it is imprudent to be too sincere to reveal oneself to others. Sometimes you are extroverted, affable, sociable, while at other times you are introverted, suspicious and reserved. Some of your aspirations tend to be really unrealistic. `
We can agree that the above can be fairly accurate to just anyone. It is a generic statement, which will trick your brain to find associations from your everyday to favour its reality. However, if this is addressed to you, you would be easily transformed to approve the description.
Astrology predictions work exactly the same way! They use simple human qualities such as:
we believe what we want to believe;
we endorse facts which puts us in a positive light;
we seek statements which tells us that we have a great deal of unused capacity; and then we shape our actuality accordingly!
These leads us back to the conclusion from a few pages before, that we all tend to have strong self-drive and we manoeuvre our lives in respect to those inner triggers.

Lastly, on the way of experimenting and finding our understanding and beliefs, it is useful to note, that we form our beliefs based on our feelings and assumptions. Emotions are the strongest drivers to lead us to our real call, it's not the act or solutions which matter but simply the way how we feel about them. Then post-rationalise it by looking out for some facts to back it up what we have already decided to believe. To change your beliefs, you need to have an immersive experience so that's something nobody can do for you. How many times did you change your beliefs due to a single conversation? Almost never! It has changed because you lived somewhere new, experienced new people and situations and it made you change as a response to those new life experiences.

You must decide to expose yourself to new impulses and circumstances which enable you to change and bring you to self-realise your set of beliefs.

Drip-Drops

Belief-system. That is your solid foundation which helps your clear judgement even when your usual support system is not present.

Have an indescribable strong pull towards ideologies or set of systems and build the application of them on a base of believing in yourself.

You will see it when you believe it.

When experimenting to find your beliefs, remember, that we form them based on our feelings and assumptions. You trigger your feelings when you experience change. Hence change will lead you to realize your value-sets.

Activities, networking and relations

I fail to understand why people do the things what they do not want to do. It doesn't make them entertained, happy, excited, either they would not benefit anything out of it, and it is not even an obligation to hang onto.

Do you tend to drag yourself into situations where you feel awkward and you ask yourself what the hell am I doing here? Welcome in the club. We are many. Yet we don't know why?

Why is it so difficult to say no to a lovely neighbour when they invite you for a fun poker party if you never play cards? Or a distant friend who ask you to join their annual pub crawl when you don't drink and hate those stuffy places? Or when your bestie goes on a holiday and ask you to babysit the cat and you just don't get along with this goofy Garfield.

I tell you why we say yes. We say yes to avoid the confrontation or the discomfort of being questioned back...oh why not? And we push away the further consequences of being unfriended by this `randomers` or being expected to apologise or be forced to say yes, the next time for an even more disliked activity.

We all want to belong and be included. Especially when we are new. In the inner circle. But the inner circle of whom?

You can say that you ride this wave and pass those minutes, saying what are few hours in our lifetime, but in reality, you are wasting your moments for nothing. The only fruit of your exercise will be another invitation for a now really getting ridiculous activity. Then another long line of such programs will slowly take up your time and fill your life, leaving no space for the real deals.

Networking is important, being social is important but you want to be involved in things and with people whom are your cup of tea. You want to embrace the time spent, feel energised and have few things out of it. I am not suggesting that you need to get into everything with a sharp agenda and a checklist of what you get out of the encounter. That's inhuman and unreasonable too. The chances are low but there, that you accidentally meet a totally random group of people and you want to stick around them. So, I am not saying that you should not jump for new things. I want you to be adventurous but smart here! Balance in everything is everything!

You don't want to be with people, just to be with people and feel good as you belong somewhere. You want to spend quality time with good quality friends; where conversations are real exchanges and relaxed fun rather than a struggle of acceptance and an effort to show to the outside how integrated and happy you are and how much you do and how many friends you own.

You know yourself, your interest and your current aspirations. When you pick your activities along those lines, that will enrich you and give you the exposure to the societies where you will feel supported, accepted and you can learn and grow. If it's not so clear, then you can even keep a log of the events where you have been to and where you will be heading to. See the pattern and feel free to rate them. There you go, you will clearly see your time wasters and your high flies!

You will also have periods when you are not so clear on what you want, or you will be already in a transformation into a new direction. For these times, you can also use a list on your desk and jot down your schedule with your remarks.

As simple as this one:

Activity	Session (1st, 2nd...)	Impression
Pole dance	*1st time*	*awesome people great music, entertaining coach even if I suffered to follow the moves, I had incredible fun*

I left the next page blank, so you can use it for your notes and if you want, you can even tear it out.

Activity   Session (1st,2nd...)   Impression

Activity   Session (1st, 2nd...)   Impression

By the impression part, use pointers, use the exact expression what comes to your mind, do not hesitate, just write instantly as the description will have huge meaning in your final decision. If the trend shows positive or negative words, that will lead you to your selection.

For example, you pick a new hobby and get into it, after 4-5 session, evaluate it. Rate it for yourself, not for anyone else. Be brutally honest and do not share your comments with anyone at this stage! If it's absolutely on the negative, then skip to the next. If you see at least 2 positives listed, carry on with another 2-3 sessions and do the evaluation again.

I can't give you a precise scoresheet on this as it is again up to your own values and only through your own lens, can be assessed.

I have few pointers to guide you however:

See how you felt when you arrived at the place?

How people greeted you?

How did they receive your comments and how they made you feel with their responses?

Did you make new contacts? Have you planned something together?

Did you exchange telephone numbers or just Facebook accounts?

Have you had some `aha` moments?

How long you have stayed with them and why did you leave? Did you leave because the gig was over, or you found an escape to leave early?

Did the time pass like a minute or was it a long painful stretch of the time?

Did you arrive home feeling recharged or drained?

Are you already looking for the next time, you can repeat the same activity?

You must trust your gut feelings.
When you need me, I meet you halfway! My support to guide you to your conclusions, will be available through our online sites.

What's your trick, your letitate?
Mine is; I can live and settle anywhere within 4-5 days. This comes with practise. If it's your first time to relocate or for the certainty, the key is that you start preparing before in advance. You can get acquainted with people and when you arrive you already have a small net to hold you afloat if you get to face few bricks or walls along. Hook up with hobby groups, sign up for activities, chat with your Airbnb host, call your future colleagues on Skype for a conference to introduce, plan a welcome party or housewarming ahead...Start networking before you make your move!
After your arrival, allow yourself some `tan and discovery` time. It is usually easier to chat and connect online, these days, anyways. People are not as open as they used to be. We are becoming more virtually social, which gives a great chance to pre-set things prior to your relocation. And one more important note here for you only. Do not make a mistake to stay following and approaching the same people. I suggest, out of experience, that there is plenty out there and the World is so rich and has so much to offer that we shall not get fixated on inconsiderate folks. If you do not manage to find a common tone, move on and endorse other groups or platforms to socially connect. Same goes for the real-life scenarios. Let me go back to one of the previous examples, I brought up.

If Garfield's keeper won't see you for a coffee anymore, just because you did not take their beauty for the weekend, the chances are high that your friend was not your bestie and was looking out for themselves only in this friendship. If they have asked few questions to see your opinion and tried to accept your no, then it is a good approach. They can show interest to see your reasoning and come up with a mutually beneficial conclusion. This is how people should work together in any relations. It is about to stay considerate and stay real. You don't need to cut the roots after one occasion like this, but you better be conscious if such turns out to be a 2,3,4,5 times pattern, then you need to leave it.

People will take you for a ride and they can become toxic if you don't set your fences and look after yourself. It is typical, when being new, that others probe you. They will taste you for trust.

Unfortunately, it became second nature to us to test the newcomers, in some cultures particularly. For this reason, it is important to stick to some healthy limits and do not let the probation turn into an abuse.

If you must fight to stay in any sort of a relationship, then stop fighting! A relationship is defined, by all means, to exist between two (or more) and for a reason! Both parties must contribute and willingly work on the relation. It must be a nurturing symbiosis, a space where both will blossom and grow!

I assume that you do not wish to chase the purple clouds with a daydream of having a friend who is occasionally filling the Wednesday after work hours to have a quick bite with you before their gym class. And you have to travel 45 minutes on the subway to get close to the gym so they can be on time...but when you ask them to come over to your favourite restaurant on a Saturday night, their weekends are already booked for the more priority friends. They have no opening in their agenda for weeks in advance and any of your other suggestions will receive a rejection also. You are The Wednesday afternoon person. And only that!

Now, the one who lives on you like this, is a parasite, a leach which will only suck your energy and drain you without any return. Or worse, will leave you with a feeling of unworthiness and press you down. Do yourself a favour! Avoid these people and look for a place where you can be the appreciated you and treated as a person, not an accessorise or means to pass time.

You are new, but you are not a fool. You are there to indulge and bind with interesting characters, build bridges and paint rainbows.

It is sometimes better to pass time with only a few precious confidants rather than pressuring yourself when trying to be up to everyone's expectations, running after relations which are born to be meaningless and a constant chase to eat up your spirit. There is no minimum required headcount, you do not have to relate to many and absolutely no use to attend activities only to keep busy every minute. Just because you are away from home, do not be afraid to be alone. It doesn't mean that you are anti-social or a looser. That`s a bumper sticker BS. You have nothing to prove to anyone. Confident and balanced people feel happy when they are just themselves too! You can enjoy different pastimes in your way, even on your own. Often when you start going, you meet the right companion along the path. You can miss out on amazing people if you never take the courage to start alone.

What is letitate?

I have mentioned this expression few pages before without an explanation just. I wanted to take you to a self-conclusion.

Letitate is a play-word, I have come up with, to express a state when one is in the flow and acceptance. In that instant, you are fully present, in the joy of the occurrence, you let it be, let it happen, let it go, let it float, let it flow and all is there to feel content and happy.

This mind-twist when applied consciously, have lifted me through some tough times. Literally turned some days, which others would call lonely hazy days, into sunny adventure-filled and memorable moments.

"Create a life that feels good on the inside, not one that looks good on the outside." [2]

Do we have friends?

We spend time with people whom we associate with.

What makes friends and who are your social buddies and connections?

Why is it important to know the difference?

Why is it good to have both?

Why should we make the distinction, and should we separate them?

---

[2]Unknown author but credit to The Truths Diary IG

Are they equal?
Are you dependent on them?
How much you share?
How much you want to share of your new scenes and people?

The colleagues from work, you invite them, or they invite you to discuss work or chew on some juicy office gossip. You go out with others from your sport or book or knitting club as you have a lot in common to share and mingle about. You reunite with old neighbours, college-mates, job buddies to get an update on your lives and to be nostalgic on old-time stories.
You are drawn to those friends by some interest, common history or some other things, you both are or were involved in.
But then you change job, you move place, you break the hobby and get a new one. There goes your group of friends too...you make few attempts to bond but there is something missing. You don't feel well being around them anymore. Or slowly they do not call you for the weekly meetups, they won't reply to your messages so quick. The enthusiasm and the intensity of the friendship is slowing. It is only a matter of time when you won't receive an answer to messages and your calls will be dry transactional chats like: How are you? And you? Silence...with great sounding promises and phases like; oh, I really missed you, we should catch up and get together for a coffee -fill the occasion with any of your usual traditions or rituals, you were doing together before.
Time has passed, you both have changed, the circumstances have changed, your life are filled with

new faces and you do not share the same interests and circles any longer. Everything and everyone are changing. You wake up today and you want a coffee, tomorrow you start drinking tea. It is normal.
Life shall be fluid like that! Not only when you are travelling.

We are human and find it difficult to release. What you must learn is to let go, move on, find progress, respect the past -you can even love it- but let it stay where it belongs, in the past. You would less likely warm up an old relationship, years after the breakup. Why would you do it with the embers of old friendships? If you still have things to share in the actual moment, then it is fine. But if it is just a nostalgic-feel and the thought of keeping those good people as you do not want to lose having them around, then it is past.
Friends are those who stick with you, no matter of jobs, places, partners. Your friends are interested in you. In the changed, crazy, happy, sad, grumpy, amazing you. All of who you are!
All my real friends are those whom I have met with no association. They were introduced to me by colleagues or those sport club friends, but they had nothing to do with me in my `role` hence they became interested purely in the real me. Not the position I filled or the common topics, we temporarily shared.
Friends are genuinely into you.
They discuss any subject with you. They listen and pay attention. They remember what you have said and remember of your opinions and tastes. They question you and intricate to develop a better sense

on the matter, they work with you in your lows and highs. They know when to speak and when to shut up. They look for you always, not only when they need you or not only when it's convenient for them. They register the events and feelings you are going through and they are participating as you need them or if you need them. You do just the same to them. They don't use the excuse to be busy but make time and find time to spend it together even if it is only a phone conversation or a Skype chat for an hour. Most importantly, they are with you, when they are with you. You have their full attention. No phone calls, no text chatting, no distractions.

It is a fun, respectful and safe place to be with real friends.

They are not around you because it is an obligation but because they have an internal drive to spend time together.

Does this sound like a good marriage to you? Well, it is practically, without the sexual side of the package.

"Friendship is a single soul dwelling in two bodies" - according to Aristotle. Although I would not go that far with my statements, yet I strongly resonate with his sentence. For that reason, I say that it is better to have one good friend, knowing that she or he is a real one, rather than having many people around, binding empty bonds.

I have been travelling all the time in the past years. It wore out many of my relations which were not real friendships. They were meaningful for a while, till we have shared the same location, interest or activities, but not real friendships.

Some days, I just craved to experience real interest, just a call or a message from someone to make me feel that I, as a person, do matter. A short text without needing anything from me and with no hidden agenda behind. Few words or a sentence in a humanly tone and with a real concern in me and only me. But such communication rarely encountered, and it is considered unnecessarily. We think if we have nothing to arrange with the other one, it is a waste of time just to ask how they are and genuinely listen to their answers.

How is it that a bit of attentiveness wanes while our daily communication is becoming meaningless? We run chats with likes, emojis, cool-yoyo comments with no content and nothing to say. It's just an expression to show that, hey, I'm here, just not much interested but keep filling me with the latest gossip or share some videos to make me pass my time in a sweet meaningless float.

I have gathered my courage and stopped those contacts. I took a stand and said: Don't talk to me only in a need of encouraging words if you don't reach me when you have good words to share.

Time will narrow your circles, let it work as a natural filter.

I have a brilliant story to share here, this will give you some insights on the dynamics of relations in different settings.

My friend decided to travel to South America, and he had planned the trip with a friend who is Spanish and was his go-around buddy for a while in an English-speaking European country. The Spanish guy, let's call him Mateo, was there to learn the language and was taking it easy, enjoying the nice ambiance of the country. They spent some time together, planned activities and invited more of Mateo`s Spanish friends to join them. It was always fun with that crowd as my friend described. They were the happy, lucky go, loud bunch, with whom you can only have crazy times. Mateo and my friend have drawn their plan to travel around for like 3-4 months and visit a few South American countries. Mateo proposed to get another Spanish guy to join them as his girlfriend was from there, so they could be great guides and give suggestions along the trip. All looked super nice and the day has come to take off. The first days of the trip were just like back in Europe, the guys had fun and immersed in the treasures of the new city which was the starting point of the round. The time came when they had to decide where next. They started to discuss the options and directions, also the timing but it was becoming more and more weary to get to conclusions. They all wanted to take a different point and the communication was breaking down. Planning became disagreements, talks turned into debates. The main crush was growing between my friend and Mateo`s friend. Mateo was in between but not opinionated. He was once staying quiet, then he changed his mind and went with one side or the other or with his own third version.

Eventually, they have decided to split for 15 days and the two Spanish guys remained in the city while my friend continued with the previously drafted plan.

He explained the situation and he was curious to hear me out. I will share with you my exact message to him:

I don't know what has happened and for what reasons you are not getting on and why you are splitting and why Mateo need to share himself between two of his friends. I can think of few ideas. Take it as a short soul-cause-searching guide or such. People change and behave differently in different life situations and different environments. It is challenging to adapt to a new place and you both can be stressed and uncertain and vent out on each other. With no fixed plan, the group will suffer the conflicts of making routes, whereabouts and how about and if you both are strong characters, then you will fight for the lead. You can be `fighting over Mateo`, for his friendship and attention and for his support...so when you suggest something you will want Mateo to take your side so that you two will be the majority and will have the right to make the next move according to your idea. Mateo can be overprotective to get close to you or you can be overprotective to let him know all your layers and shades; the buddy relation worked in Europe for party going and stuff but now locked together for larger decisions and for 24/7 is too much and he or you or both find it too much and exhausting and don't want to be this close. In Europe, he had to rely and depend on you while now maybe you have to depend on him due to the language. You might not like to be dependable and he might don't like to be the one to guide or help others. Whatever the situation is, now you were given 15 days to be alone to think and immerse in the beauties of the places! Finally, they have never reunited during this trip. My friend found occasional travel companions along his route and did and amazing round.

The Spanish guys remained in touch with him, but the sense of friendship between them was no longer questionable. They knew they were good buddies back in Europe.

As I would say; Tie the knot where it strengthens the string not where it's needed to hold it together.

Everyone should read the Subtle Art of Not Giving a F*ck from Mark Mason. Not because it's ground-breaking rocket science what he exposes, but because his conclusions brilliantly can lighten us up from all that stress and stiffness, we are living in. People are just taking themselves too seriously and can't be natural and human any longer. Interactions are not desired and being together seams a hassle most of the time. Ultimately what we desire and what makes us happy, it's the exact same thing what brings us problems and labels our challenges.
Every good comes with bad. Take each encounter for what it is or was.
Some relations have a short lifespan to serve you with some experiences. It is more often than not, that you will only know the purpose of an encounter just way later. It can come to you as a sudden realisation, typically.
Some connections are meant to be there for longer and for a lifetime.
Generally, when you travel, your relations will be very intense and fun, but they will be short, sometimes as short as the length of your stay in the country.

You keep meeting the same spirits

The name, character, nationality and appearance will be different, but the core of the person is just the same.

It gets even more scary when you realise that you are a magnet of the same souls. Your closest people turn out to be born on the same day or even in the same year.

I was sitting with my writing buddy on this extremely beautiful and unusually warm Golden October day. We were at his home place, a small village in the mountains of South-Germany. It's so well tucked in the Black Forest that I would have difficulties to spot it on the map or to find my way back. And I have excellent orientation. Normally if you drop me in a new place, I see it once and then upon the next return, I could recall all its shapes, streets and locate the sites easily. The place stays on my mind as a visual photo and I just see it from above like an aerial map and even years after, I can remember. Not at this time. But geography is not my main point here. Let's get back to the main scene and lose the magical forest scenery.

So, we are enjoying the day and discussing many topics and as the days go by, I am getting more of those chills running down my spine. I have known him for a bit longer than 4 years. We have met here and there, did some trips around, yet this is the first time when we spend full days together. This is the time for long meaningful conversations and to realize how much we are different and still have tons of things in common. These chill moments are becoming frequent guest during the chats. It is when you sense that you know this sentence, this reaction or the way of expressing, from somewhere. I have spent the first days contemplating on the feeling and did not bring up my observation to him. Finally, during star-watch, I have asked for his birth date. For a moment, I could not believe my ears and then it all came together. Bam, he was born the same day and month as one of my long-time best friends.

Here it goes the adventure seeking stubbornness, the productive laziness, attentive loner-dreamer, adrenalin junkie who always and sharply knows where the zig-zagging roads are leading him.

Everything is easy and he does all just naturally and with no hesitation. The surface is a very individual characteristic and strong charisma, yet deep down, he carries roots which are plugging him into my circle and making me feel connected to him since even before birth.

Unbelievable how I have found these guys on the two opposite poles of the Globe and both by chance.

It is not a single time, this has happened, but it was the most recent and intense encounter hence I'm sharing it with you.

While traveling being for a short trip or for relocation, you will meet a lot of people. And only the real matches will stick. I would reassure you that wherever you go, you find good people and attract the ones whom are on your wavelength.

It is you. The magnet. As someone once said, wherever you go, you always take yourself with you. And the same type of people will be attracted to you as elsewhere. Feel free to go where your feet take you and stay relaxed that you won't be alone! You are surrounded by the same souls along any journey.

Distance relations

And here I am not talking about long distance romantic relationships. There are plenty of theories and discussions around that topic out there, no need for another one.

I want to discuss when your friends, family and cool buddies are spinning the party some thousand miles away while you are everyday hustling in a totally different setting than at home.

How does it feel when your bestie snap-chat you from home, they have the party of their lifetime, all your friends together and you are sitting alone washing down your frozen meal for one, with a large glass of water? Or if you drink than replace water here with anything you like.

Not cool! Trust me. It can go as far as depressing -brr how much I dislike these negatively charged words; they give me goose bumps- if you don't do something about it! And I know that you will! So, let us get going!

I will discover two paths here with you.

One, where we handle your right now distant family and friend's affairs.

Two, where we make our future distant friends and acquaintances plus the aftermath.

1.

You got separated. It is painful. It is bringing up a burning need to maintain your life back at home yet, you can't rot at home like a lettuce in the sun and wait for their updates. If you do so, you are going to go nuts! Nuts! Nuts! Nuts! No, not almonds, walnuts,

peanuts, pecans, not even macadamia! Doh! I am talking about a state where you lose yourself more than Eminem was describing in his song and you can go way further than Forest Gump when he jogged around the Globe.
You want to avoid such scenarios, so do yourself a favour and go on reading a few suggestions here.

Sometimes I was sitting at the Guadalquivir river, in the South of Spain, looking at an entire sunset through my phone screen to register every colour and every sunray. I haven't seen the real version of it. I was busy recording. I was glad that I will be able to share it with my loved ones and give them a nice moment or two.
In reality, how often do we look at a long motionless video? You admire the first 10 seconds, possibly speed browse through it-that you do to see if something happens in it at all - and leave it to become history. With my attempt to register the whole event, I have missed the moment and my friends had received a fairly meaningless captions, with my best intentions.
Other times I would go to visit some places just to show it to my friends, just to make them happy, as I knew they would like that place. The idea to cater to their taste and fulfil their dreams by me visiting their bucket list places, was again a good attempt, but only worked as a drive to get myself out and about. In Seville, I have tried to live the days of my friends back in Malta, thinking that I have a connected social life. It was a gimmick and not fulfilling at all. At the end of the day, I was roaming alone in the most beautiful and friendly city in Europe. This was a town where

everyone would talk to you even when I just sat for a coffee or did my walk from work to home. People are open and genuinely into making new connections. Ideally, I would have gone with those hits and make new allies. I was busy being somewhere else, in my mind. Lesson taken.

I will help you a bit to live a great and social new life in any space, yet keep your loved ones integrated in your every-day. You won't lose sight of them in good or bad. You need to use technology to administer the events, they enjoy together and to show them your new groups and activities as you like and as much as you like. I suggest not to aim to share literally everything. While being connected is important, oversharing can become a burden on you to enjoy your new social circles and you will miss out on being present while you keep recording, Skyping, commenting, picture sharing with those back at home.

You can end up not being part of either. You realise that you have attended an event and only seen it through the lens of your camera or the screen of your mobile phone, Yet your friends back at home did not get to enjoy it with you, as they only got a cartoon-like wiggles of the whole experience.

When you drag on with your motion pictures, you may bore the one sitting on the other side or piss them off by holding them up in what they were doing. It can also happen - unfortunately and rather rarely, with real friends- that your other half turns green and yellow, and boils in jealousy, and won't take your calls again.

My best practise would be to enjoy the act and share

later. Capture all the heart warming, funny, crazy, blood pumping moments and then later when you are back at home, share it to all whom you wish, could have been there and would have greatly fancied it.

Share a little but with deep meaning. Summarize. Add personalised messages and captions. If they are hooked, they will ask for the story telling.

Do it sensibly! Even when sharing after the event, do it with the intention to cheer up the other when receiving it and not to an extent that it can strike a different reaction.

2.

New people. New places. Unknown habits how they relax.

It is different how people relax, what they do in their free time, how they do it and with whom? Where they go, how much they are willing to involve new people and how you will not feel as an outsider?

From the inner circles -friends, family etc- to the peripheries and how to land back, do we want to get back at all?

Do we want a strong, deep bond everywhere where we go or a friendly handshake, share a glass of red relation would do?

Our expectations, our social needs will decide what type of relations we build when we are starting somewhere new. We can decide to keep the new connections casual, enjoy a good conversation, share things and then walk out once you move away. This can save you a lot of pain and headaches. However, it is not always a choice and certainly not a clear cut.

Do we want colleagues to become friends or we want to separate work mates and play-buddies? In my opinion, it can only improve your work relation if you give a chance to meet your colleagues outside. You watch out to pick a suitable activity and just go for it. You can go with different work – groups and do not be afraid that you might join a less popular division; it doesn't mean that you will be locked into that pocket and you won't be able to mingle with others.

When I landed in Cyprus, most of my co-workers were good 50+, then a bit of 40+ and one or two of `me`. The team was not exactly acceptive at first, they had great doubts what a 24-year-old would do for those whom are experts in their job for over 20-30 years?! I did not foresee any out of work social activities with them when I even had few walkouts on me during team meetings. It took me a few weeks to understand the intentions of the group and a lot of effort to hear them out and make myself at least heard. They were a bunch of amazing people with incredible stories and savoured to a level that calling them wise is an understatement. Would you have expected that such a diverse age group can assimilate and share common topics while enjoying bonding activities? I didn't. Their approach was totally different than anything I knew from before. They were a very closed group, who have been together for a long time. They were not ready and maybe not interested in anyone new. They have monitored me and gave me the cold treat. There were even a few tests here and there. Many of them kept asking the same things and most probably they have shared if I was giving the same answers. We had small challenges with the language as well, which I resolved by learning few useful sentences and used it even if I could not pronounce them. Being correct was not the object. Communicating and connecting was the matter. My aim was to keep approaching them, I did not show my disappointment for any push back and I did not wait for them to reach out.

I was lucky that one of my friends is from Cyprus. I have met her in Luxemburg at the Small Nations Games. She sat next to me and my coach, wearing her Cypriot national uniform. It became obvious that she was listening to our conversation, but I did not get it why as we were talking in Hungarian. Then suddenly she said with a perfect delivery: hey are you also Hungarians? Our jaw dropped. Turned out that her Mom is from my country while Father is from the island. So, when I have moved to Cyprus, we reconnected and started to spend time together. She has helped me a great deal to learn about the local habits, introduced me to a few of her mates and the language. She was my first association before I would have become part of the group of my more seasoned colleagues.

Surprisingly, once I was accepted by them, the intensity of social activities turned out to be much more than with other age-groups. They really have dedicated time to have fun when meeting up. Daily, we have shared breakfast and lunch time, we went to grab food after the shift or do the shopping together. At times, they even have cooked for each other and brought it over. I really enjoyed sharing time without much pre-planning. They were spontaneous and integrated friends into their everyday normal activities, involved their families and being all together was not a big deal, it was the norm. Once one was included, was part of everything and anything. No hassle to pick the place, time or define the duration. You could join in and leave when you wished without a need to make an excuse. Not only the time spent was very intense but also the communication. They talked of worthwhile topics and came to divinely interesting conclusions. It looked to me as a very mature and close community and it was one of my best times when I could be a part of it.

How to approach groups or how to find people with your current interest?
In Cape Verde many of my colleagues had a current interest to kitesurf. It is not necessarily their main interest in their home setting but in this new place, we were staying at, they wanted to find those wave-runners to learn from and hang out with. And where else to find them then on the beach? They hit the coast and found the gear rental, chatted up the locals to find instructors and through one person they were led to the other to then slowly integrate themselves into this new lifestyle group.
It can be done the same way with any of your interests. You need to figure where you find the people practising your thing and you must go there. You can search online, ask colleagues, I even used to drop a short question to random people like the waitress in the restaurant or the barista at the coffee shop.
Do not think that I am such a chit- chatty one! It takes me great effort to start a conversation. Although, there is one thing I have developed over these years

of travelling. I observe who has a friendly outlook and can be open to be asked. A genuine smile, few attentive words or a quick handshake gives them away. So, I hunt for those approachable folks and grab my chance to connect or get some useful advice. It happened that some I have asked, practised my hobby and even invited me to join their group. When you have gathered few pointers, there is nothing more to do than just go there. Yet again, spot a sympathetic candidate and converse. I find it best to use a simple filter. As I do not know them, but I know myself, I take myself as the measure and choose someone who acts similar to my behaviour. In a couple of minutes, you will be able to sense the roles in any group and if you look well, you can start seeing the characters. If you are a generally a shy person, do not try to go and hook up with the noisiest person or the one who is in the middle of the attention of the act. You have a low chance to bond with them and you might feel pressured to talk to someone who is not your cup of tea. This can then ruin your first impression and entirely turn you back from joining the group.

Expats or locals?
For me it was mainly the question of the language setting. Where English – or any of the languages I know - was not widely spoken, I would find and spend more time with expat groups. However, it is also a factor if you wish to blend and expand with the local traditions and habits, or you are seeking to spend time with those who share similar experiences and cultural background as yourself.
The latter is surely lower effort but often less

enriching. And why to travel if not for the personal evolution?
You can guess my preferred choice now.

You can start with different groups and then the circles will shrink or lead you to even more new faces and eventually you get a nice crowd, with whom you can spend great times.

What picture you want to project about yourself? You do not want to stay the low dog, but neither be remembered by a ridiculous topic or super embarrassing statement you drop.
Do not try to be different with the aim to be accepted. Be yourself. Otherwise you won't have fun and the connection won't be real.
What to say? Prepare with topics to avoid anything offensive or too memorable.
Ready, steady, go. Gather your own icebreakers!
Please remember, that it's never a matter of `your message`, but how you think of it, and how you translate it into expressions and what emotion it generates in you and eventually in others. You need to consider that the language you use might not be the first language neither for you nor for your chat partner. Certain statements can be misinterpreted. Try to avoid very picture -like and complex sentences at the beginning. It's better to be simply understood then all-roundly misconceived.
If you want to grab attention, speak to the new friends in their language, use communication vessels like handwritten notes or even music. Make it playful, make it fun so they pay attention and the good feeling, you have given to them, will stick with them,

so they will be encouraged to come back for more. I observed that often people start with a rather hostile approach, then they watch the opponent like lions do, they measure and scale their position compared to the other and then they change the mock-up.

Genuine kindness, humbleness will open doors in any situation. I see many hotel guests approaching the reception with a grumpy face, full of disappointments from the first part of the trip and judgement of what's coming up next. When they face a warm smile, a great pace and being shown interest to comfort them, they turn 180 degrees and become best friends with the person attending them.

To be received positively, you may demonstrate the same behaviour, in any new encounter.

How to stay tuned with these people and if you want to stay tuned after your departure?

One thing is certain, that you will agree to keep in touch after leaving. And you pass those nice `I stay writing. Sure, we keep in touch. I'm going to miss you` tears in the eyes moments...yeah right!

It sounds very well but try to stay in touch with every single person you have connected with, and you will never have a waken moment when you are not chatting or phoning up someone from your past.

You can have one or many ways how to handle communication from the distance. I have a simple take on this subject. We have few catch ups and we share when we see something that reminds us of each other or gives us a Deja vu of what we have shared when we were together. I do think of them very, VERY often as they are part of me; who, why and how my personality is today. Every time you meet someone and connect, they will take or make a piece of you. For that reason, it is not how much you communicate but the feeling you have for each other. If you are connected, you can go for days, weeks, months not talking and yet carry the same resonance for each other.

After years have passed since we have worked together, I still get messages, addressing me as Boss, Queen or Dearest Friend. It touches me deep. Very deep. I feel it straight in my heart. I do not fancy these titles and don't take them by the meaning of them. I do love them and enjoy them indescribably. It is not that I want to be called on these names to feel stronger or better than anyone or be the big distant respective person. Exactly the contrary! When I'm given these precious names, I feel the connectedness. I do not know for what reason they have chosen their words and picked this one or that one. And there is no need to know. Maybe they felt me like that. Or this is how they see me for the moment of the text. The real reason doesn't matter as it doesn't exist. It is still how they wanted to call me, on that impulse and such emotional charge doesn't pop from a place of the mind but only from the heart. It makes me believe that I could give them something so different that had shaken up their World and they still carry me in their mind heart or soul and feel me close. It is the hope that they might get some strength when remembering me. It is the thought of our time and talks together that makes them be a little better and push a bit further. It is our learnings and sharing which keeps them on the go and nurtures their dreams and the journey to lead them there. When I see a message like this...I look up and breathe deep with a smile. I send a thought to the person who has texted me. In that moment, I know that every single second was worth the struggle and I am grateful for all of it.

I love the crazy ride and the great people I have met along the rollercoaster so far.

When it's time, we will meet again. Even if it's not orchestrated at all.

Don't think of your travel and distance as a dividing factor but more of a bounding glue.

We condition our mind that distance in space also means distance in heart. It is you who makes it so by deciding which relationship can and which cannot survive on an A to B point difference and a long-time scale.

Why is it so that your parents will always be there or your sister or your brother or your cousin?

I know what you are thinking, family, your blood, right? They must stay and stand behind you. But it is not evident. They do not need to be there for you. And you don't need to be there for them. It is also a mutual choice; you make this bond or break this bond.

I want you to look in the mirror now and honestly answer this question!

How often you meet your friends who live in the same city? How often do you call or text them or check-in with them? How much effort you put in to make it happen?

Distance will show who your real connections are. As

if someone wants to be in your life, they will be. And they will make all the effort to stay, no matter where and how far you are.

In these times when we can be more connected than ever, we are more distant than possible. And it's not the physical distance that creates the gap. It`s us. Our choices. We rather post something impersonal and seek approval from total strangers and chase likes and momentarily fame than ask a question from a beloved one in person. We make a conscious choice and opt for the one-way communication as it's less confrontational than a real-life discussion. We prefer to hide behind chat boxes and social platforms so we can create our picture perfect. We don't bother to mould our self and deal with the people we should most care for. And as long as you stay behind the big curtain of your well-designed stage, nothing leaks out, nobody knows who you really are, not even you. That's the real tragedy, which brings some crisis on when facing some unknown, being home or abroad.

People want to seem strong, hence they choose not to talk about the emotional aspect of relocation. It looks like a weakness to discuss about, rather we bury it inside. It's in fact a very important topic if one wants to be able to happily live on.
You must learn how to detach yourself from the old and how to connect to the new. And do it all the time when you change place.
Even if with the help of technology, you can be part of the happenings back at home; time difference and physical limitations will make it just painful, as you will see them but won't be able to be part of the events, won't be able to live it, experience it.

You can be a spectator only and long to be there.

   I wish that you dedicate time, effort and energy to consider all the aspects of your move; learn to connect and disconnect when and how it is due and feel free to talk it out if you face any difficult feelings.

Today's plan: tomorrow.
In hard times blossom.

Drip-Drops

We are becoming more virtually social, which gives a great chance to pre-set things prior to your relocation.

Real contacts are valuable. They can bring you closer to your goals and help you to fulfil your personality! Others will only fill your time and waste your energy.

The better the network, the better! Yes, I said that! Go for the groups where you have your head and heart.

Cliché but you can learn something from everyone! Every opinion will widen your horizon. Hear them out but remember not everywhere you fit in is where you belong. Do not cling in there.

Get out of toxic situations. You are new but you are not a fool. You are there to indulge and bind with interesting characters, build bridges and paint rainbows.

Build your expectations and attachment according to the nature of the relationship.

Friends are genuinely into you.

Generally, when you travel, your relations will be very intense and fun, but they will be short, sometimes as short as the length of your stay in the country.

It is you. The magnet. I would reassure you that wherever you go, you find good people and attract the ones whom are on your wavelength.

While being connected is important, oversharing can become a burden. You can end up not being part of here or there either.

Don't think of your travel and distance as a dividing factor but more of a bounding glue.

Accept yourself

You take yourself anywhere.

When you travel, you are not only having a lot of impressions and observations, but you hear and get many comments about yourself too.
People will tell you how they see you. They will form their opinion according to their perspective. This is obviously influenced by their backgrounds, so on the distant corners of the World, you will receive various comments, delivered to you with a different approach. It will be all about you but from their point of view and filtered through their subjectivity.
You will listen and observe. But you should not change who you are by people's expectation, to be accepted or to follow what you hear from them as an advice.
Do not go where the wind blows you!

Naturally, once you have left, you can never go back.
You can never be the same person again who departed.
Your knowledge, your ideas, your habits, all will be changed and changed forever. New ways of thinking, new impressions, new associations. It will have an inerasable influence on you. The new place will be part of you now. Every trip will enhance your personality. You cannot take everything with you and can't behave the same in various countries and continents; you won't get the same reactions; you can't even express yourself the same way; you will have to do some deep learning on each trip and

adapt your act. You must yet preserve and protect your identity. That is the core of your character. Your unique awesomeness and energy inspire confidence in others. Some people make you laugh a little louder, smile a little brighter and live a little better. You are the trigger, do not let that blur or slip away.

How can you make sure that you stay true to yourself and protect your identity even while absorbing fresh ideas?
How can you get to this fun spot in a shortest time and with the least pain?
We look into the possibilities together!

Giving away your spirit and mind

Let's paint a picture of a nice evening when you invite your friends over, and you want to serve a lovely meal to them. You clean the flat and set the table and organise all to feel wonderful. Then you start preparing the meal. You want to impress them so much and give them your very best. The appetizer, the soup is all ready to detail. Then you hold the kitchen knife and carve out a nice chop of your own calf, the best lean meat you have on your body to serve up a delicious steak.
Are you standing there flabbergasted and thinking that I went nuts, saying yakk this is crazy even just to picture?
Well, yes and no. You want to give your best, so you give a piece of you. Ridiculous! That's oversharing. Why do we still do that with our spirit and our mind then?

94

It's your norm that you watch out for your body's safety and you seek a certain level of security in everything you do. I am wondering why you would only care for your physical body's safety rather than your sanity and mind`s peace?

The other end of the scale, where you would not be concerned about anyone but you. You strongly believe that your personality is impeccable, it needs no internal drives or outer motives to be shaped and you despise anything you hear about you. On one hand it is a good path to protect your identity however it also isolates you from all the beautiful enhancements and learnings you could absorb if you have stayed open.

Selfishness is a disease of these days. This society teaches us to master selfishness and nearly expect it as a toll of success. It's incurable unless we do realise and consciously do something with it. Our parents grew up in socialism and strived for the welfare of the whole and all. The new generation, all the XYZs are coded to grind and earn the well-deserved individual triumphs for oneself! Which is not a bad concept. Unless the win is over few others' total failure to such extent as the loss of their life stability or sanity. The walk to the throne is paved with their deadly sucked bodies and the one taking the crown, fails to see the path leading up to where THE One is. And such epiphany is a life of a mayfly yet grand and super-over-rated desired!

What is the solution? How can you find the golden-middle? It's good to play with such thoughts when you have some time, but I give you a tiny tap on the shoulder type of advice on what to do with this situation.

Well, my practise and advice is to start with yourself. Discipline yourself to dwell from within; Stay open to welcome ideas; Select them carefully and by your own filters; Demonstrate balance and uniqueness; Live by it, live for all and with all; Then spread this sensation. Every day at least to one and then to another one and do not stop living with the whole in mind. When you are slicing the cake and thinking to drop the knife and keep it all for yourself. Just don`t! Be disciplined as much as you are disciplined to breathe and sense. Be a cheerleader for the very new version of One for All, All for One idea! Star your movie and be the musketeer of your neighbourhood, of your workplace, of your sports or social clubs, your evening school, your friend's party, your cousin's city and your region and your country...be as big as you can imagine and you can be! Be a unique superstar in the new era of integrated All! Don't struggle to get, to have, to be. Don't swim against the currents. Float. What's yours it will be. What's not yours, it won't happen. Be calm and content. Aim to feel satisfied, grateful and relaxed where you are, and love to be with yourself. Seek no others to complete you, to feed your soul, to fill your space and time, to make you be `someone with them` or to make you feel needed and understood. Choose to be with them to share and collectively grow. This should be the goal to achieve such feelings and deeply believe and live by it. It's egoless and selflessness. It's a state where you are ready to accept whatever flows to you to enrich you and make you be who you are meant to be and how you were meant to live. It's not a monk wisdom, it is not an old mantra. I am talking about a weightless state where you will enjoy every waking or sleeping breath, you notice the beauty what surrounds you, dare to say and act how you may please without offending or hurting anyone of course - else if you do in this manner then you are selfish prick, period - and you appreciate the people who truly love you. Love you. Not the reflection of themselves in you what they love. Not the slave of their needs, wants, expectations. Not the shape of them with you! Explain this further! Yes, I do. Let me, please! We like people whom are like us or the ones whom we want to become. We find comfort melting in them and not needing any effort to make them understand our ways, means and beliefs. You will not need to lengthy explain your thoughts to a like-minded and no debates will occur. You amplify the same words and as it echoes, it becomes your anthem which you can sing together, and this feels good and cosy and reassuring. Every human seeks reassurance. And no conflict. And strengthening.

How does all the idealistic points about integrity lead you to stay the unique you and accept yourself? It helps you to ease up from expectations and allow to see yourself in a realistic and balanced way. In that state, you can realise your own ideas, needs, wants and desires at the beginning. Take that as a grand zero and allow progression. Question yourself, your reactions and behaviours. The more encounters, the better! It is hard to say out loud what you think of who you are, but it is necessary for acceptance and

97

then for progress.

I can't tell you exactly what you need to do because each journey is individual; yet I give you a few of my tips and examples from my experiences, so you might use them at first until you have your own style.

Doatest!
Paper pen go.
I need 3 names. Your best friends right now.
5 attributes what makes them your best friend.
Do you also carry those attributes? Or do you wish to acquire them?
It's great, that we have cleared this out.
The short exercise brings a good insight and helps you to know yourself, as we pick people who are like us or we progress towards being like them.
It is not to look for yourself in others or want anyone to do anything for you to make you, you.

I like to point out extremes, please allow me to explain an interesting twist here.
Someone would try to use you to see themselves in certain ways. They would cling into you to enjoy how you look up to them, how you compliment them, how you make them feel better and give them a new impression on who they are. And they not only enjoy it but also provoke it. They only like you and need you to feed their ego and make them someone they do not want to invest energy into becoming, but they want to get there instantly. I recommend not to hold onto such a comrade.

Last year, on New Year's Eve, my buddy told me that he rather spends the night with his new group of friends which he feels deeply associated with. He said that they are very nice and naturally warm people and he felt that he finds himself or his cure to find himself within them. I was happy to hear that he is happy and ever cheered him! This also meant that I was ditched. LOL. Ugly truth but it looked like I had to pass NYE without a planned-out companion. Which I was happy to do so. I can roam around and bond with random groups and faces and soak in more of.... what's called ...social studies while observing `peoplez` and `groupz`. I have a lot of fun doing such. I don't have this feeling of aloneness at all, I always find nice acquittances.

He was sceptical of my idea and challenged me. Then he got hooked on the alone thing. He asked what am I running from? Why I enjoy being alone and how it makes any sense to stay moving at a pace how I did / do. It was hard for him to get my concept of being restless, footloose and so ever curious that I crave new stimulation all the time. I live for the people, experiences, new surroundings, new impulses and new feelings. I discover myself through the conversations I have with those new faces around me. Some are moments of joy, fulfilment, realisation, learning, embarrassment, shyness, greatness, fearless, free and flying, some are deep rooted ever lasting friendships.

When he asked, I long contemplated on it. Okay, at least for an hour or so. And realised that he doesn't have my lens. I truly appreciated his challenge as it has led me to more realisation. I understood him, yet he doesn't have the same experiences as me, hence he can see this living in a very simplified way and interpret it differently.

People are projecting on you trying to tell you who you are and your place in the World. When facing those whom are strongly opinionated, it makes you confused because your signals are telling you that that's not true. Grasp the boundary and stick to it. Prepare yourself for such an environment and use boundary bubbles where only the good goes out and the good comes in. It protects you but allows you to give the good out and receive the good. Take your ground, start to know yourself and live the moments!

Persistence is key. Keep repeatedly doing keep practising and then nothing can stop you, the strongest force is within and the deepest source is if you know who you are and who you want to be.

We are more than capable of change. For that though, first, we must accept a realistic picture of ourselves. Maybe my intense travel and meeting with many people, have speeded up the process of having ideas who I am. It can be my take for this moment and can be partially a conclusion for a lifetime. Either or, I can say that I have learned to accept and protect the state as it is and do not let my flaws weigh me down.
I work on me.
It's a great project and as long as you want it to be.

For instance; I hate and love myself when I forget something, and I know that out of precaution or of my OCD (Obsessive-Compulsive Disorder) everything must be hyper-organized to the second. I don't make notes about things, thinking that I will remember, as I have this abundant computer-like brain...well not always. Exception makes the rule, right. And then the dilemma comes, of course, always in the worst time. In these moments, you realise that you can't know yourself enough to predict everything and control everything. The opposite!

I love when I fail, when I lose control over something because these make me stronger when standing up from there. I love when it's not perfect, when it slips, trips and makes me fall. I love to realise that life must be lived and cannot be driven through with a tight grip on the steering.

These thoughts came to me when I have lost the pin of my credit card, because I have a couple from different countries, and I couldn't memorize them. I was in the supermarket, standing at the counter with all the goods packed in my bag. The most embarrassing moment. I can't pay. One card won't pass, for some reasons it's not compatible with their payment system, and the other, I have no idea of the pin...I have nobody here to call, don't even have a local sim to contact the bank abroad, as I'm new. I could have panicked but whatever I would have done, it would not have changed or saved the situation. So, I took a deep breath, excused myself and offered to return all the items to the shelves. Apart from the emotively strengthening takeaway of this situation; on the spot, I also made a promise to myself to always carry some cash when going to shop.

Here is a show of self-presentation, a moment of fame, which goes well with knowing and presenting oneself. Undoubtedly a typical hotel story.
A man comes up to me on a bright sunny morning.

His face is red. Unfortunately, not from sunbathing.
He has asked for the top manager, the one in charge
of everything, the decision maker. Those are his
words. I haven't even reached him yet; he runs to me
as he sees me next to my colleague. He catches me
on my lower arm and drags me straight to the pool. I
managed to escape from his grip and showed my
hand to him to introduce properly as civilised people
do. He is not accepting the handshake, just starts to
scream from the top of his lungs. Everyone turns
head to see him. Even from the balconies. Suddenly
the pool deck looks like a theatre scene. He is saying
something surely, however, all I hear is unacceptable
and that we have ruined his holiday which he has
been saving up for the past year and he cannot relax,
and it is unacceptable, and it is unacceptable and
unacceptable and unacceptable. He goes on with his
speech for a good 5-10 minutes without letting me
open my mouth. His finish line is that, now he must
waste his time speaking with me instead of enjoying
his vacation. Well, I did not talk a single letter yet, he
could have kept it shorter and returned to his holiday
activities. I have asked few clarifying questions to
understand, that he was upset as he didn't get his
desired sunchair on the pool deck. He demands his
stay to be offered for free as `we allow other guests
to reserve the sun chairs, when they only leave their
book lying on it for hours and they sometimes won't
even return`. It is unacceptable that some people
occupy the chairs when it is against the pool rules
and we must enforce this, and we are responsible to
keep the area clean and remove the things from the
chairs. With the same breath, he also explains to me,
that the day before, he left his used pool towel on a

102

sunchair, only `as a sign` that he is coming back after lunch and a nap but the pool boy had removed the dirty towel due to that, he has lost his sunchair. And it is unacceptable. And we do a very poor job. Especially the pool boy, Farad – his name is Femi, but do not mind. Very poor. When I have offered him few alternative solutions, including another set of sun chair, 2 chairs next to the discussed one, he refused. `It is clearly not what he wants and in a luxury resort this is unacceptable`. He suggested that I go and deduct all the charges from his bill and invite him to spend the rest of his stay all complimentary.

It was an hour or so to come to a common tone. We have chatted and as a final closure, he told me that he sits on the loungers just next and I shall send them at least 2 free cocktails for the inconvenience.

Why do people like to nag about things more than sharing nice things?

How people can be so bad that they behave outrageous for a 5$ coffee or a cocktail? Why they treat someone so bad when they do not even know the person?

Is it about the complaint or is it a power game to boost their ego and self-confidence or to make them feel superior when their life seams flat? They might be lost and want to be somebody well known, even if it brings negative reputation, but reputation. They got the two seconds fame and will be remembered till the end of the holiday. Is it worth it? I don't think so. Better to work towards knowing who we are and how we are. Not to aim to score popularity with a toll of such bad connotation.

In the process of self-discovery, you can use practically every experience as building blocks. You can take something from everyone and from everything – like all those countries where many nations lived and left their heritance and it shaped and coloured the lifestyle and the culture. It made the grand identity of those places!
There can be good and bad, a mix of both. They can lead you to start defining your identity which then will be your strong base, your grip while travelling.

Travelling alone

Everything what we have created in this World was first created in the mind. Whatever we once made up in our heads was manifested in this reality that we live in today. For that, magic is science we don't know yet. And we can cook our own.
It is not a fairy-tale. I am only referring to the endless opportunities we could notice and absorb and the way how we make a selection between them. Both the inner work and the building must happen.
Travelling alone can do a lot for you in these regards. And mind you, I'm not a heartless lonely wolf to roam around singly. It happens that I travel alone by choice or as an assignment.
We tend to think that we do not always get to choose our lifestyle. According to my humble experience, it is not the case. We pick the first option, then life flows with us, your hunger for knowledge and to help others grow and carries you forward, more opportunities are presented to you and new paths open. The rhythm captivates you and you realise that you start making decisions according to this type of

set-pace; it becomes your life and if it was another way, it would not even make sense.

You always have a choice and plenty of opportunities. The question is, if you are open to notice them or blinded by your expectations and usual settings. It is not easy to widen your horizon if you are lost in the noise of your everyday environment and a prisoner of your contact`s opinions. However, travelling alone is a great way to find your direction and silence the outer voices to be able to listen to the inner one. Many of you will tell me off now and say that it is not fun to go to places alone. You will say that it is awkward to sit in a coffee or restaurant by yourself and it is pointless to be out when you can't share the experiences with someone else.

I see it that the purpose of any venture can vary. It can be shared fun or to take time for yourself. Then the experience will be exactly how you think and feel about it.

Let me tackle the awkwardness first as I feel this is the main reason why you would not make plans alone. Then other concerns will be debugged along my story too.

I have had a very busy season in London, and I felt to struggle for a breath of fresh air and sunshine after the gloomy city days. I managed to take 6 days off and all I was craving is silence. Silence in and out. To hear my thoughts and not those of others. And not the commands. Not the expectations. Not the must dos. As all my friends have worked in the hospitality industry, we could not arrange to travel together, neither had the time to plan a lot. I got those 6 days and had to make a move otherwise I stay stuck in town. I went home and scanned the skies, found a ticket to Mallorca, rented a car, and booked a hotel on staff rate. It was all improvised and done in less than 20 minutes.

It was going to be my first holiday completely alone. This time, I was not flying over to visit a friend, not meeting anyone on the other side. I was heading out to spend 6 days on my own. I did not have time to contemplate on this fact.

On the day of my flight, I started to stir a few thoughts in my head and questioned what exactly I was doing. I felt weird on the plane already. I thought my co-travellers are staring at me, being on my own. What a silly thought when they would not even know that I am holidaying alone…? Still these were my feelings as the thoughts I have planted in my head. The plane landed, and I was busy getting the rental. Very lucky, I was upgraded by one category and received a nice Smart. Started to head to the hotel and kept myself occupied with the scenery. The warm weather with the sunshine made me happy and I felt lighter than ever in the past few months.

The accommodation, I have picked was an old hacienda, located in the centre of the island, nested in a huge vineyard with all its antique glories and green bushes. It was a blast and I pleasantly and slowly started to ease and forget my worries of travelling alone.

Until the check-in. The lady just popped the question – Are you staying alone? – I am. Thanks for the reminder. She did not mean any bad with her question. It was even a standard and simple question without any implications. Yet, due to my previous mindset, I felt that she was pinching me and addressing me as a looser to come out there on my own. I shook of shame and kept looking practically anywhere else but at her. – I could give you a beautiful upgrade, this garden suite is spectacular, I hope you will like it, my colleague will show you there. Oh no, she even pities me so deeply that she gave me an upgrade to make up for my loneliness! I was sinking. So silly! Instead of appreciating this grand gesture, I mumbled a quiet thank you to her and followed the man who was carrying my luggage. We have walked through a lush garden; it was smelling like a citrus fruit basket mixed with some flowery notes. The sight was more than what I could describe. This building has smooth arches all around in down-toned sandy shades and some nice colour patches added to it. The decoration is all natural. Plenty flowers, bushes and crawlers on the columns. The outdoor furniture is made of hand-sculpted iron and cushioned with bright blue, green and yellow fabrics. The sight is breath-taking already which took off my mind from my self-pitying.

The voice of the Spanish man breaks my momentarily meditation. He might have been talking even previously but I was into the surrounding and did not register any word he might have said. He kindly opens the door and points me to walk in. Is this my room? – sudden thought hits me like the lightning. Hello, I got an upgrade and just realised 15 minutes later. The helpful porter explains the layout of the suite and few important information, then he asks if he can assist me with anything further and politely leaves. I probably spent half an hour going in circles in the room and enjoying the views over the vineyard. The experience now overwrote any previous assumptions and I felt very happy and settled. I started to get hungry though, it was time to get to a restaurant. The hunger served me as a useful drive to get out and on my way, I even made it back to the reception to thank them for the amazing room. I got in my little supercar and being with myself, made me start a new chain of concerns. How does it look to go out for dinner alone? What will they think? How is it perceived that a woman goes to a restaurant without company? What if they do not even give a table for one? What will I do while waiting for the food? How the others will look at me? I began to consider other alternatives. Stopped in front of a supermarket but did not get myself out of the car. Am I really going to eat from the supermarket just because I am afraid what other people will think when they see me sitting alone? Ahh no, nobody really cares or looks around. I drove further and parked in front of the seafood restaurant, I picked earlier. It is a small place, directly on the seaside in a village suburb. I took a deep breath and walked in. The owner was at the door, welcomed me and asked me if I needed a table for two or how many? I gave him a smile and answered that it will be just me at this time. He smiled back and led me to a table on the side and just on the seashore. Either he understood that I would prefer a more intimate corner where I can comfortably hide or he instinctively gave me a good table, no matter of how many we were in the party. Reflecting, now I am certain that it was the second case. He gave me the menu and wished me to enjoy the dinner. I fixed my eyes on the menu card and did not look around much. Down on the menu or up to the sea. My eyes were moving between the two safe points. My face must have been red as if I would have had sunburns. I felt shy and really embarrassed when I had no reason to feel this way. It was a wonderful place with warm people, and nobody actually bothered to look at me or take notice if I was solo. It was only me who had the idea to hide and shame myself for coming out alone. I was sure that everyone had noticed my singleness and will make a comment or few thoughts about it. How silly! If I was someone famous, they might be looking but why anyone would look out and discuss a random stranger. Everyone is busy doing what they are doing, dealing with the things what they are dealing with and I am certainly not the topic of any. It must be the ego to make us believe that we are so noticed all around or maybe we wish to be. I made it through the entire dinner without any further dilemmas. I have enjoyed the great food and the owner have passed by to cheer me just as he did with all others. It was a good experience and all in all, I was busy indulging in the food and the views. To your biggest surprise, there were no questions if anyone was joining me or if I want to wait for someone. They did not pay more attention to me than to the other guests in the restaurant. I was alone, enjoying and that was all to it. I was proud of myself for breaking through my shyness and allowing myself this nice experience.

In the morning, during breakfast, I grabbed my book and used it as a safety fence. This was my solution and worked well to distract my mind from overthinking my imaginary `tough` situation. I hooked up with a nice elderly couple and exchanged a few ideas what to see during the day. I was set out for a full round around the island.

As the days have passed, I begin to care more for the sights and adventures and much less if I had company or not. I was deeply into the emotions this trip had triggered in me and had made few realisations on what's next when I will be back to London.

I was always surrounded by people and could easily share when and how much I wanted. At the same time, I had the luxury to turn inwards and dwell in sweet silence. I was interpreting what I see in the way how I really encountered it and could pass it on as an original conclusion. It became my time and I really eased up. By the third day, I was so used to the solo setting that I didn't even have a slight thought about it.

What has happened? Suddenly nobody was gazing at me or questioning me? Not at all. The same comments and standard sentences were there. Every time I have passed an attraction entrance, sat in a restaurant or ordered something, they have asked exactly the same way if it was for one or anyone will join me later.

It was not the voice which had changed. It was the eco.

In my head there were no more doubting thoughts. I have accepted the `soloness` as a fact and switched to enjoy what I have come out for. I have turned to the one person whom I certainly live my whole life with. Me. And it was a blast. To be with me and collect beautiful moments and translate them for memories and let them trigger further thoughts.

How is it possible that we are feeling shy to take a trip alone when normally, we prefer to spend our pass-time in solidarity?

Why do we need a distraction to be comforted?

I am also learning how to do nothing and yet not feel embarrassed about it. One of my practises to look at people on the metro.

It's a long car, like one anaconda snake zigzagging under the streets of Paris. I notice all the heads down. All hands busy. Fighting with the phone or some reading. Nobody would look up, not even when someone sits next to them. They do not even move. People need to be engaged all the time. They have an urge to do something in every minute, to distract themselves from the surrounding and pass the empty time. In their own micro space, their own matrix. Why we cannot just be and why we need to reach for our phone as soon as we have an empty minute? Why can't we look around and saviour what surrounds us? Is it embarrassment or what's the feeling and why we can't look at others or just chat them up with few questions? Even on the metro or on the train, you would keep yourself engaged for every minute as if it was so shallow to sit and watch. I feel that we forgot how to let time pass by and how to just be. In those moments, you breathe, and you sense what's around you. When you do that, you also start to see new things and experience the World around you. That's when your brain gets new impulses and you can start making up new connections between things and persons. This simple 5 minutes starting can be a daily exercise and give you a totally new brain circuit and perception-set over a short time. When you stare in the World, you will stare at people. And you learn from them. You observe their looks, their speech, their tone, their mimics, their reactions, their body language, their behaviour between each other.

I do this very often and more often than rarely; it teaches me a lot to see what's going on outside me. I use expressions like outside me on purpose. I want to emphasise on the fact that you also need to get out of your shell if you want to enrich, or when you are looking to discover than accept yourself.

Everyone feels more or less comfortable being with themselves. There is no conflict, there is no rival and it's a pretty lukewarm cosy spot to be with yourself. It is a standard statement that you will have your personality formed, when you are grown to 21 years. In my opinion, you should keep conceiving and shaping yourself as long as you live and willing to do so! Most of us are scared though to carry on with this evolution and just want to get it done and dusted. So after, your wrongly and now close-squarely shaped personality, can be blamed in any conflict situation or your upbringing can be the fault why you can't handle certain situations. It takes energy and effort to continue moulding and preserving yourself and requires some level of bravery too. You need to face your deep dark corners and at times you find few skeletons in your own chest. Finding them is a beautiful discovery but the journey only starts there. That's the trigger for you to then look at it, learn and experiment and eventually decide what to do with that old dusty piece. Do you want to polish and cherish it, or it needs to go?

You see and meet people who can show you new ways of looking at things, they can demonstrate

approaches which you have never heard of and can shake you and wake you. There will be positive pointers which you will want to integrate in yourself and there will be the negatives which are great lessons on who you do not want to be.
Both experiences are must and well needed to evolve. Once you start looking outside of yourself, you can sense these impulses.
I had encountered very strong affections and was clear that I needed them in me and then less evident ones where I was taking my time to chew them and evaluate them. I have used research, readings and heard out friends and family on the questionable traits.
At times, I had such a shock, seeing my own negative attributes in others that, I immediately could cut them by the roots and never looked back.
However, the gardening is your job.
It is your odyssey to build, mould and keep your identity.

Character is everything who you are. It is ever complex and ever emerging. The impact of others on you will be as strong as you allow it and they won't change you, only if you want to absorb them. For this reason, I encourage you to get outside of yourself and start seeing the World as it is for you! You must do the things you think you cannot do.

You will have many questions; concerns and you get into debates with yourself. It can be painful and can tear some relations apart. Your friends might not understand the new personality traits you just developed, or they will no longer be interested in you once you have sent your ghost back in the haunted house. When we change our lookouts, will our behaviour and speaking also. Your family and close ones must know what you are going through so they can be prepared, and they won't have a shock when day by day they find a `new person` sitting at the kitchen table. They must ride the rollercoaster with you. Only then you can be a success as they will facilitate your experiment and support it rather than provoking.

How easier it is to carry on living with a so-called shaped personality!

I am not here to live between my four walls though!

Do you want to get out of yourself to get to know yourself?

Do you want to see the World exactly as it is...well through your lens?

Are you still up for it?

I share an ever-simple silly exercise, I did. Such can help you to sense the people, behaviours, characters and maybe find something you wish to add to.

Please don't laugh out loud! Or laugh and `Just do it!` [3]

I have picked a warm spring day to sit on a bench in a busy touristy fishing village harbour. I had no other agenda than being there. First a Chinese guy passed by, he asked me to take a photo for him and chat me up for like 15 minutes. He told me about his life in Norway where he lives for 5 years with his family and how he learned the language and he liked his job as a hunter. He said that he enjoyed talking to different

---

[3] credit to NIKE lol

people and he finds it very interesting to hear about their life. He also asked for a few touristic tips and restaurant recommendations. He invited me to join him for a meal. Before he left from the bench, he took a photo of us as a memory and headed to the suggested fish restaurant for lunch. Then a French couple came. The lady looked a spiritual one with her Indian caftan looking like trousers and hippish hair style, the man was classy in black patent shoes. They were eating strawberries, they also took many pictures of the harbour and talked softly between them. They sat for probably 10 minutes and then left. Then an old British couple came, the woman smoked, they murmured a few words and then the man said that he was hungry, so they left. An Indian young couple, in their traditional outfits, followed them, the man set on the far edge of the bench and he invited the wife to sit next to me. She looked at me, I smiled back at her, then she turned embarrassed and told the husband that she was not tired so she doesn't need to sit.2 minutes must have passed by and the man held her hand and prompted her to keep going. Then an elderly German couple came; the two women hugged each other and smoked a cigarette together. She kissed her on the cheeks and told her to grab a coffee before they leave on the bus in 20 minutes. My last bench buddies were another old German couple. They had not stayed more than 15 minutes but carried on with a constant soft chat and shared some fruits and a bottle of water. They were the only ones who sat quite close to me. The others kept distance.

I gave you a factual report of this exercise without explanations or conclusions. It is to serve you one idea on how simply you can get out, stay quiet and enjoy some enlightening observations without seeking for any camouflaging distraction. At the end of the day, if you may please, just be at it and enjoy, no need to make instant deductions for the first time.

Footloose in life, observe as much as you can, allow your intuition, dreams, believes or whatever you call them to guide you, follow your inner voice and consciously pick from the outside influences. The gardening is your job.
It is your odyssey to build, mould and keep your identity.

Your type of work and company

I have succeeded in eleven countries on three continents, turning things over for a big hospitality corporation and got my crazily positive and passionate self nearly few burn outs. I dedicated my drive, my knowledge, my skills, my ideas and my creativity to the benefit of a big enterprise. That same big company which let me go without a say goodbye, after nine years of full commitment and multiply successes with the teams. I started to feel, I was held back from learning and stack in the frame where they have locked me. It seemed that I'm wasting my days. `If you are the smartest person in the room, it's time to leave.` `When we stop learning, we die.` these were running in my head. When voicing my thoughts, I ended up leaving with the final sentence from my boss: `if you are not happy, get the fuck off! `So, I did! It was the best instant and instinct move; I could have done for myself!

I was like a jolly joker; they could land me anywhere and we have succeeded. In the multi chains` rigid operational frames, you get your guidelines, policies, procedures, suppliers, materials and trainings, all from the shelf. You shall travel with that survival kit, compiled by someone who possibly never worked in your role and rarely faced a guest; while trying to climb and conquer some Mount Everest. You constantly need to find the gaps for your creativity, the little cracks in the wall, where your idea might fit in and passes; changing the blood flow of the organization. I felt huge progress in me and around me. We cheered and celebrated each other and appreciated every opportunity to gain knowledge. Still, for my leaders, I remained the `never enough in something or for something and the need to learn more about this or that` person. Despite my `amateurism`, I have been approached by the same bosses to teach and support few new top executives, as they were newcomers to hotels and to our brand. I was being looked at as a young woman, stereotyped down to, not to have the capacity to control and lead globally. There were never-ending promises for my advancement and ever-adding responsibilities and tasks which were made part of my actual role. I was happy to eat up the challenges and acquire and I looked at every angle and absorbed things which were not even part of my game. I was driven to then use all the know-how and integrate it to advance and give an edge to my people. Every time, I have tried to discuss my leaders` plans with me, they always said, it's not a race it's a marathon. It doesn't matter whoever takes the credit for the results, as long as the company succeeds. As I understood, smart and confident people will not try to impress with overcomplicated big words; it is about clarity, not to stretch things! All the jargon they lengthy explained, sounded wonderful, but in reality, it was a piranha` pool. Once you have tried to progress, the food chain was slowly digesting you; you as a person, you as a team member, you as a contributor, you as a human being...all was getting dissolved in the political acid.

In such environments, when you got no game, you can only get advanced with hard work. I outworked them. Not necessarily working harder but working kinder, more attentively, keeping up to my words and focused on the most important at a time. That's the path, I have walked. I know that it is not the pattern of least resistance, however the knowledge and the experience through sweat and tears will be yours and nothing will erase it.

I have achieved a lot with a young age, adjoined amazing people and learned plenty, yet I did not feel accomplished. I strongly felt, if I stay, I will be pushed to change in a nature, I did not wish. For these reasons and with the last kind kick of my ex-boss, I choose to continue the learning process on my own; went to look for more and new.

I see the past twelve years somewhat clearer now. I am grateful for all the knowledge and to get to know the people I am honoured to be connected with.

At times when I feel nostalgic for a moment, I long to go back. This crave quickly passes and I return to

reality to notice that I am better off to choose to be who I am and lucky to do the things fulfilling me.
I might not have concluded all I could have done in the hospitality industry, but.
Would the toll have been worth the reward?
NO. Surely not. I am glad for my intuition, guiding me to weigh where I stand and let me let it go.

Life and business have circles and it doesn't have to be always full.

Wanting is one thing.
This is a short sentence which most accurately describes the period which followed my resignation.
It was a debate if I shall return to my profession, take on a new direction or pursue something on my own.
Returning to hotels was the first dissed choice. I have burned the candle from both sides and exploited this field as much as I could. I did not have the interest or the intention to start anew in the same era.
As the first attempt to take on a new direction, I have applied to job post where I had nothing to do with the required expertise however, I felt that I would love to wake up every morning and do the job.
According to what I thought the work was about, I was certain, I had all what it takes to rock it. Guess what? I got my Dream Job!
At least that is what you would like to read here. But my Dear Reader, that only happens on social media or in some other catchy script where one would try to sell you a life changing course at a greatly slashed price and only if you sign up instantly.
The thing about truth, that it will still catch you the

next morning.
So, I woke up and moved on to the next idea.

Finding a job was not the best match for me at this stage of my journey.
However, I would like to still give you few hints how to approach this topic. I encourage you, not to feel forced to stay in any position if you steadily experience stagnation, boredom, fatigue, loss of interest or simply do not fit in the company culture. I know exactly what it seems when you are a thousand miles away from home and you think you depend on that job. You don't. You are not there for the mission only; you are there as you choose to take off and travel abroad. You have established a life there and now must have some sort of a safety net of few people to rely on. Your support system will be your thoughts, ideas and your drive to change as well. There is nothing worse than sticking with anything that drains you, only because you believe that there is no other option, without even giving it a try. Use your resources to ask around, browse online, contemplate on various options and if needed find a head-hunter or a coach for advice. You should not settle unless you are satisfied.
Intelligence is the ability to seamlessly resolve problems, knowledge is what we gather through kindling our natural curiosity, literacy comes with reading and relentless learning while awareness is a matter of will to seek and absorb information and extend our perspective. In that sense we all have abundant potential to grow into anything. However, it all comes with effort and resilience. It's not an overnight trick to find your professional call and just

jump in without any preparation. Success is 10% inspiration, and 90% perspiration.
Agility looks for what is known to solve problems. Creativity looks for what is unknown to discover possibilities! Use your creative energies when hunting for your career-direction!
Don't keep a shark in a pound! Scale yourself to the right job, don't go low. Build and carry such self-respect and confidence, not to accept undermining offers. You may say yeah right but who is paying the bills then. I will just take this one until I get the real deal! Flat out! I assure you that after years, you will still be sitting on the same chair and paddling the same boat. You will warm your chest on rainy days with a promise to yourself that you go and find the right thing and then use the excuse of busy and no time, not to do it ever. I understand that it is extreme, but you must do it for yourself. Or you can use a simple trick if you must go low. Go as low that you can't optionally stay in it. It is a project, a part time job, a casual summer internship. It is a gig which naturally have a collapse date which will keep your arrow tight in your bow. So, you will be looking instantly and immediately as soon as you have started. This can be the only way. Trust me. This advice can save you miserable years and the breaks in your career. And you don't want to experiment with these. Time is your capital, your most valuable asset, do not let it go wasted!
Catch your what would have happened moments, and your what would happen if moments? These are worries of the past and the future, both are not available for you right now; they are time wasters.

How is your perspective on your possibilities? Do you feel the abundance for your future, or you have a scarcity approach?

Your perspective will determine what you believe is possible for you as Sháá Wasmund greatly phrased it. In many family stories, we can find a proof of this. Take one of my regular guests who has shared the story of his sons. He is humongous successful in politics and shines in public fame. He has twin sons. They lived in the same house, ate the same food, wore the same clothes, got the same education until high school, were being influenced by the same people and experienced the same events in their lives. One grew up and followed the father's path, got one degree after the other, won awards and at a young age, became involved with politics. He is a stunning man with charisma and in the spotlight of the top intellects. The other brother skipped college and went to travel the World with his casual friends, those vultures feeding on his rich ass. He is an alcoholic, a drug addict and enjoys public fame for his ridiculously lavish lifestyle, supermodel affairs and supercar -hotel - restaurant - concert accidents. They are both settled in the way they are. They live by their perspectives, filled the void in themselves and used the bits of the given jigsaw to build their own puzzle perfect.

The World is...how you see it. The key to success? Keep going until you feel well, find your audience and your voice.

You are programmed to pick out what you want to hear, what's familiar, what you associate with. And ignore the things they don't fall into these categories.

This makes it hard enough to put through a message. Imagine when the receiver's perspective is being ignored. Such mess in communication can break your future work relations and career. Clear, two-way communication to mutual understanding. This could be the first effort when finding the right work- match. It's the essence for you to fully understand what the job, you fancy, really entails. This delivers key insights for later evaluation.

So be concise, clear and blunt when passing on your message and check if you have the same understanding with your listener. Same when your future boss, colleague or prospect talks to you about business. Look out for the common ground and get each other properly. Use self-worth instead of self-confidence, when negotiating! *Practise being the last one to speak* -as Nelson Mandela suggest- let your partner to say what they need to say and then react with the facts at hand.

A new job is like a new marriage. Happy pink clouds at first and then the rain starts. If you did not study in advance, it can be too late once you are already in!

You may opt to start your own endeavour and establish a small one-man show venture or a company, depending on who and how you wish to serve and what that field requires to run.

You can find your passion if you play a bit with this thought: If I had everything, I have ever dreamed of, what would I be interested in?

World peace, educating the next generation, bringing pure values back into the everyday, leaving a legacy for all, taking meaningful actions to enhance societies, helping individuals to be at their best and

be their best!?
Choose carefully from the listed activities and see where you can best utilise your strengths. Think of all the activities, you can link to these motives and see what can be useful to a potential customer or built as a structured and demanded product. Do not focus on fame and money at first.

We hope that success will make us happy. We are mistaken when thinking that and surprised than when after being praised, we still don't feel good. It is because the external feedback is half as strongly persuading as our internal beliefs and remember that we only see what we are looking for in the World.

Not everyone was born to be a CEO, entrepreneur, doctor or rocket-scientist. Choose your heart's desires and your lifestyle match as you will spend a great deal of time with work! Consulting and running your own business are like being interviewed for your dream job every day!
The work you do, must reinforce your nature! An introvert cannot be a great salesperson; can be a success for a while if they put themselves out, but not for a long term as it is not who they are and how they behave, think or operate. They possibly do not have the ego to keep going after rejection or failures, but they have such warmth to stay human that won't allow them to run much after business.

List 3 things what you like in yourself;
Mention 3 good happenings from today;
Say 3 things in your life what you're grateful for.
You may mention random or ridiculous things yet,

this is your perspective through your own lens! And these are much stronger than any external influences or drives. The list you just made, can be a good base to play with different directions or to find professional targets. It can work as a strainer when establishing and evolving your business. Keep in mind: *Mastery is a moving target. No one builds a legacy by standing still.* I love the slogan of the luggage brand, Rimova. It is an ever truth, nicely put.

Finally, if you are more of a visual person, you may draw a map where you have all your highs and lows, your strengths and the things that you wish to work on and the end of your treasure hunt! And follow!

Don't die with your music still in you. Find your right fit! Even if it takes time! Don't go for anything just to do something!
Being able to live as an expat and work abroad is not a restriction to cement you to one place. It's a privilege and a huge opportunity. Use it like that!

After all these discoveries, allow me to conclude with a poem which always reignites me when I feel heavy on my feet and or in my heart.

"All that is gold does not glitter,
Not all those who wander are lost;
The old that is strong does not wither,
Deep roots are not reached by the frost.
From the ashes, a fire shall be woken,
A light from the shadows shall spring;
Renewed shall be blade that was broken,
The crownless again shall be king."

RR Tolkien

Drip-Drops

You should not change who you are by people's expectation, to be accepted or to follow what you hear from them as an advice. Every trip will enhance your personality.
You must yet preserve and protect your identity. That is the core of your character.
Discipline yourself to dwell from within.

It is your odyssey to build, mould and keep your identity.

Character is everything who you are. It is ever complex and ever emerging. *Always be a work in progress.* – Emily Lillian

Footloose in life, observe as much as you can, allow your intuition, dreams, believes or whatever you call them to guide you, follow your inner voice and consciously pick from the outside influences.
The gardening is your job.

We all have abundant potential to grow into anything. However, it all comes with effort and resilience. It's not an overnight trick to find your professional call and just jump in without any preparation. Success is 10% inspiration, and 90% perspiration.

Your perspective will determine what you believe is possible for you. - Sháá Wasmund

When everything seems to be going against you, remember that the airplane takes off against the wind, not with it. - Henry Ford

Love and more

Life is simple.
Love relationships are simple. There must be two in synchronicity, with the will to walk next to each other, look in the eye and never down or up, hold as strong as one needs a grip at the time, project love, care and respect towards each other, strong enough to tear down the walls of their ego and make anything work for the two!
As soon as one decides to enter a relationship, they decide that there is us from that moment so with every thought, act, word they should open their shatters and consider to co-exist and cooperate with the other. Ego is the biggest enemy of any relationship as it does not allow one to listen, to observe, to accept other than their own opinion and their own truth. And the couple which shall be one unit, suddenly becomes two opponents, competitors, contenders working against each other fighting for one's truth, when there should be just THE truth for THEM, if there was a common will to make things work. Anyhow, in any circumstances, at any time...just make things work. Simply. Keep each other happy in any possible way.

Your partner - if you are in a relationship and privileged enough to stay at the same address - will be the friend with whom you share every awakened moment and even when you sleep.
We already have spoken a lot about friendship and relations when you are constantly on the go. But what happens with love? It is already hard enough to maintain the connection with your beloved ones,

how can you establish a love affair or keep one going?

The lucky ones start to travel with their spouse and their agenda is mainly to nurture the bond while on the road.
Mind you, it is just as emotionally and spiritually demanding as holding a long-distance relation in flames. Their physical distance is not restricted, which makes things slightly less complicated as communication will remain fluent and in person. Yet, when you change your living environment, you are surrounded with unknown impulses and non-familiar scenarios will continue arising.
If you are entering this situation being in a strong relationship and a likely willing partner on your side, the transition will be easier as you share the weight of the upcoming challenges.
In case the relationship is shaky; the trip can really speed-kick it into two opposed directions. You may realise how silly you have been acting over small, unimportant matters and you bond stronger than ever. Or the other radical solution will be a crush break up and separation as the new setting will hit both of you hard and you will be served plenty trials to realise that your differences are greater than what can be worth to work on.
Very often, one from the couple, would make a larger sacrifice to join the relocation. I have seen this happening. Those guys were happy at the beginning of the journey until facing the first hurdle. The ones giving up their life back home, would start to feel the weight of their decision. Often, they blame the other for being pushed to let their good life go for

something less worthy or satisfying. You will not be able to avoid all the hard debates, yet such a blaming thought will only come to you or to your partner in case if the relationship is already out of balance. This becomes the cherry on the cake and blows up the hot, dividing conversations.

I suggest, to weigh all aspects before agreeing to change location together and only move if the new place is suitable to the both of you. No grandee gestures to be offered or hard sacrifices are to be made here as they never result a settling outcome. I know what you are thinking, that a mother or a family man cannot leave the partner and kids behind. I say, they can. They must. When they both have something valuable going at different localities, the age of the kids is crucial to change school and social groups, safety is a concern, or the extended-family support is indispensable; long-distance relationship can preserve a healthy family life opposed to moving together ending in collapse.

The game plan must be laid out clearly and in advance so both parties will know what to expect. The strategy must include ways to maintain intimacy. This was always a crucial point mentioned by the separately living couples. You better give those flames before your spouse would go off and look around to find it somewhere else. If you are having a hard time to pose in front of your camera and record yourself, you should ask if this second of awkwardness can be changed to minutes of pleasure?! Place the whole scenario in a different context and turn your attention towards the person you are doing it for or virtually with. You will get inspired and now your passion can be passed on and will be felt even when your partner receives the message.

I can ease the cluelessness with few messages here; `I'm standing on the top of the cliffs and staring at the morning lights playing hide and seek on the top of the ocean. The air is sweet and heavy. It`s filled with the ripe smell of a mango and papaya with a hint of cedars. I feel the force of nature and all that raw energy flowing through my body and I'm synced with nature, I become part of it. Then I hear steps. Stepping gets closer and closer. A warm palm touches my waist and cuddles me as naturally as if it was coming to its home-place where it belongs. I feel breaths on my neck and a soft kiss to comfort me, that I'm safe. Your body softly touches mine and frames me completely from the back. Your arms are now wrapped around me. Your breathing takes the pace of mine. My pulse picks the rhythm of yours. We are in the sweet mould of `us`. `

`Can you make our life as elegantly smooth and pure as a waltz, as passionate and intense as flamenco, as playful and fun as salsa, and so steamy hot and always surprising like reggaeton? `

Do you see it fun now? It's playful and you can make it exactly to your own little shared language and likes. You can include scenes of your new place to further describe it to your partner and to show them how they remain part of your thoughts and days.

Oh, one more tip: use secure channels to ensure that the special moments remain shared only between you two. My additional suggestion might sound trivial for long time couples but for the newbies: only do it

132

with someone you trust that they won't expose or shame you.

Transparency is key in any long-distance relationship. It scores even higher importance when the relocation is for a long time period. The couple shall have a full plan when to visit each other, how to holiday together, how and how often to communicate and what to share through which platforms. Many of my colleagues lived apart from their families or spouses. Some used fixed times and days to have Skype chats, some agreed to text every morning when going to work and sending a small video report on their day every night. Some preferred to run a small written end of the day story, including pictures and a weekend life call. I had colleagues flying home every second weekend and the family visiting every last weekend of the month. One of my office mates had a habit of waking his wife and kids with a video call. We knew of their `rise and shine` ceremony as he was doing it in his lunch time from his desk to match the time zone back at home.

They all have shared their sorrows only when the agreed communication channels and methods failed, or the said traditions were not kept.

It happened that one of the girls was used to have a good morning WhatsApp message from the fiancé. One day, he had decided that he sends her a romantic email with a poem instead. She stayed gazing at the phone screen, leaving the application open and waited on the message. She recited many horrible options for not getting the usual text. She had called him up. He was driving to work with no reception on the metro and unable to get her calls. She had sweated and teared up until he finally rang her back. The momentary mystery was solved. The relationship temporarily tainted. He had the best intention to surprise her with something special, yet it had freaked her out, not getting the usual greeting through the agreed channel.

Doubt and uncertainty hurts. However, knowing that your spouse or family is safe, and all is going well; balance can be kept, even when long miles away from each other. In our times, it is so easy to connect, we can be part of anybody's life even on the other side of the Globe. It is a privilege and shall be used in the most suitable way for you.

Some stories were chanted about hard decisions such as moving away when you have just met someone or relocating again when you have found your partner in your new place. For me this tends to be the most twisty situation. The relationship is fragile, and trust might not be fully established. You do not know each other enough to plan ahead and sometimes even expectations can`t be laid at a very early stage. You might feel that you have found an extraordinary person and you want to be sure that you keep warming to each other even when far away, yet your other party can be totally against the long-distance idea. If someone at the beginning would try to stop you from moving, only because they do not want to try for a remote relationship; run. Take my word. Do not ask why, do not try to find an excuse for them, do not think how sweet it is that you mean them so much. Just don't. Move.

If your spouse from your new location, is not willing

or due to commitments, can`t make a move with you, you can see back at the beginning of the chapter, how you can build a strategy to continue the relationship on the compass.

Depending on the time you have already spent together, you may work on alternatives with your new partner. For me the essence is trust and mutual willing effort. Without it, a remote relation will never stand a chance and will scare much more than pleasure.

I do not want to come up with a lot of vague kumbayas and not here to convince you to have faith, yet, I say out of experience, that you must not postpone to take a stake or have your move on hold just because you cannot go apart with your newly found partner. If the connection is there and you work well together, than there is no distance, issue or other parties which can possibly divide you two. Distance can`t be a question between two strong people whom are linked like the two opposing poles of magnets. Even if it is not love, not the classic framework. It can be an unexpected meet and click. You do not need to talk all day every day but when you do, reflect deep connectedness and send each other vibe as if you were always near to each other. It is as the quote says: *"You can't go as far that I won't be with you"*[4]

I have a poetic example on expressing deep affinity, let me share it as I really like the passion felt between these lines:

`Love me at your deepest, hate me at your darkest,

---

[4]From Vaiana, a computer animated musical adventure film, produced by Walt Disney Animation Studios, in 2016

argue with hot virtue, romance with smooth waives, warm me with your heart's hidden secrets, doubt us for better, challenge for the brightest future, teach with experience, be wise when in a moment of lost senses, cuddle for safety and let release for personal space and our freedom, hit me with all the spectrum of emotions, thoughts, moves, reactions, hit me with the raw YOU. Let us both be ripe and deliciously imperfect`.

What happens if you transfer your single life to a new place? Can you find love, or will you have to pass days without intimacy and compassion?
I know for a fact, that your lifestyle, interests and goals for the move, will all define if you allow space for someone in your new life. When you are moving for a career advancement and you stay focused on work, go out rarely or only for formal gatherings and rest at home alone; admittedly, you lower your chances of meeting someone. And it is by choice. If your lifestyle leave space for fun, you keep practising hobbies and mingle with versatile faces, you set a good ground to bump into Mr or Ms Right. Better accept that you have little control over the time factor of this matter, however, if you stay open, the opportunities surely will line up.
Are you staying long enough to invest in building a relationship? Further questioning won't lead you to straight answers. It is your personal choice what you will get out of your encounters. You can enjoy and play, you can aim for long term. Drive the situation to wherever you may wish to be. I would like to make our World a better place by small contributions. One of them will be this message to you, my dear reader:

whenever meeting someone who catches your attention, stay true to yourself, do not do something what you won't do back at home; be fair and open about your intentions. We have seen enough heart breaks and ugly games.

Long term is absolutely possible, and you can score your lifetime partner, if that is what you are looking for and you do make some efforts and attempts to meet people. Here the key is to stay on the lookout. Ms or Mr Right will not come and knock on your door.

I have been to many weddings of friends who have met while both expatriating. Recently, my Hungarian friend, with whom we have met and became friends in Malta, had married her Australian fiancé, whom she met while working in Dubai. After the marriage, they have decided where to settle, now together. They live in Melbourne.

In an interesting movie, called Collateral Beauty, they say that *"We don't get to choose whom we love…"* So how does this happen then?

How can we foster a more loving approach? Psychology professor, Arthur Aron explored whether intimacy between two strangers can be accelerated by having them ask each other a specific series of personal questions. The 36 questions in his study are broken up into three sets, with each set intended to be more probing than the previous one. The idea is that mutual vulnerability fosters closeness. To quote the study's authors, *"One key pattern associated with the development of a close relationship among peers is sustained, escalating, reciprocal, personal self-disclosure."* Allowing oneself to be vulnerable with another person can be exceedingly difficult, so this exercise forces the issue.

The 36 questions that lead to love.

Often, I wondered what stops me from walking up to a sympathetic stranger, start up a conversation and not sound flat boring. Perhaps I lack what to say or ask – this is common to many people nowadays, and that's where this guide come to play. You just need to know the questions to chip in at that beginning to connect, get closer and possibly win the stranger's heart. I am sharing this set, not only to be as a tool to scout romantic love, but as an icebreaker set of questions to generally connect in any social situation and build alliance.

Set I

1. Given the choice of anyone in the world, whom would you want as a dinner guest?
2. Would you like to be famous? In what way?
3. Before making a telephone call, do you ever rehearse what you are going to say? Why?
4. What would constitute a "perfect" day for you?
5. When did you last sing to yourself? To someone else?
6. If you were able to live to the age of 90 and retain either the mind or body of a 30-year-old for the last 60 years of your life, which would you want?
7. Do you have a secret hunch about how you will die?
8. Name three things you and your partner appear to have in common.
9. For what in your life do you feel most grateful?
10. If you could change anything about the way you were raised, what would it be?

11. Take four minutes and tell your partner your life story in as much detail as possible.

12. If you could wake up tomorrow having gained any one quality or ability, what would it be?

Set II

13. If a crystal ball could tell you the truth about yourself, your life, the future or anything else, what would you want to know?

14. Is there something that you've dreamed of doing for a long time? Why haven't you done it?

15. What is the greatest accomplishment of your life?

16. What do you value most in a friendship?

17. What is your most treasured memory?

18. What is your most terrible memory?

19. If you knew that in one year you would die suddenly, would you change anything about the way you are now living? Why?

20. What does friendship mean to you?

21. What roles do love, and affection play in your life?

22. Alternate sharing something you consider a positive characteristic of your partner. Share a total of five items.

23. How close and warm is your family? Do you feel your childhood was happier than most other people's?

24. How do you feel about your relationship with your mother?

Set III

25. Make three true "we" statements each. For instance, "We are both in this room feeling ... "

26. Complete this sentence: "I wish I had someone

with whom I could share ... "

27. If you were going to become a close friend with your partner, please share what would be important for him or her to know.

28. Tell your partner what you like about them; be very honest this time, saying things that you might not say to someone you've just met.

29. Share with your partner an embarrassing moment in your life.

30. When did you last cry in front of another person? By yourself?

31. Tell your partner something that you like about them already.

32. What, if anything, is too serious to be joked about?

33. If you were to die this evening with no opportunity to communicate with anyone, what would you most regret not having told someone? Why haven't you told them yet?

34. Your house, containing everything you own, catches fire. After saving your loved ones and pets, you have time to safely make a final dash to save any one item. What would it be? Why?

35. Of all the people in your family, whose death would you find most disturbing. Why?

36. Share a personal problem and ask your partner's advice on how he or she might handle it. Also, ask your partner to reflect back to you how you seem to be feeling about the problem you have chosen.

Love. This well is an ever-spring. These are beautiful words, not mine though. It's an old proverb from an unknown writer. I got inspired when reading it and a short brain-pour started.

`Love is simple. Love is easy. Love itself is effortless. Relationships are hard work. Love does what it's meant to do. It draws the right person, at the right time to you. The person who will challenge you, lead you to fulfilment, looks after you to become your best version while they also become their best or make you feel better or worse for the better...and love you exactly as long as it's meant to serve you both. Every love makes you realise something different. Every love feels love. Every love is a lesson to be learned. Every love is a unique feeling. Every love lives within. Every love shows you you. Every love reflects them. Every love can be with one only or with many. You can live love with one in many ways and many times. `

It's a desire people all have. You and me and all. We dream of a big union. To be one with another one. Even if we all know that it's not possible. There is where me ends and where you start. There is no melting together and forming a new mould. And even if there was, it would not make any sense in our humanly simple existence where everything has an end and a defined form. You can't simply imagine otherwise. Me either. Our brain limits us, and we barely can make up something of the unknown. Whatever we build in our fantasy, is a collage of the known, we have soaked in throughout the awaken or the less conscious times.

We use the cliché of two half finding and completing each other. This statement feels so wrong. A half cannot function and, in that state, cannot find a suitable pair to work towards each other's best. You don't need someone to complete you, you need an independent strong complete to share life's best with and evolve together. It's two individuals going into a relationship with the only agenda to seek better for the two and not with the sick dependence to use the other for self-completion.

We don't fall in love with the right person. We fall in love with someone who is right for us at that time. Everything is temporarily like a sandcastle and needs both the rain and the sun and a lot of work not only to be built but to keep it up if it's worth a lifetime. *Parallel lines will never meet* – as Sadhguru explains in one of his speeches- don't look for people exactly like you, with the same ideas, beliefs, plans, vision and the exact same life. With differences, you have a chance to bond and grow together when at points your paths are crossing. It's an exciting and fulfilling journey what every relationship is meant to be!

What do we wish for in a normal relationship? What is normal? Nothing is normal. Each relationship is different and has its ups and downs and comes with all the hardships and daily difficulties. At times you want too much and nobody and nothing is enough to provide to be satisfied. There will be always more out there.... more desired... if that's how your attitude is towards your relationship. When is it time to choose? When is it the one for life? Never! The only thing is to decide to settle. Go for it. Stop looking further or elsewhere. Turn your energy into that relationship what you have signed up for. Feed it, nurture it and as you do, also work on yourself to be the best partner you can be.

I was taught to unconditionally give and raised to keep my closed ones nurtured and looked after. People nowadays can't do that as they do not trust that such investment is worth as they do not see or expect long run relations. While in the old times it was evident that you will stick to those around you for a long time, so dedicating your life to someone was easy and based on trust.

I am lucky to say that I have witnessed many wonderful relationships. Starting with my grandparent's marriage. 67 years. Still counting. Still happy. Seriously, I get tears in my eyes when my grandma tells me what a good man my grandpa is, what an exemplary father and excellent partner he is, and she is blessed to have him in her life. They hold hands, look at each other with sparks like teenagers and attentively and gently care for each other with any little gesture all day and every day. When I ask my grandfather, what is the secret of such a beautiful marriage, he says, that you need to respect the relationship and work very hard in it. He said that you don't get a day off. It's one happy 24/7 shift.

I was supposed to discuss love and relocation. Again, why am I starting with the smart-sounding generalities?

Only, to show you how deep you shall allow yourself to fall, that you carry yourself into any relationship and yet even in a romantic one, you shall preserve your identity. Especially while abroad and feeling a bit more needy for companion and intimacy.

It is soothing to immerse yourself into someone and enjoy shared moments however losing yourself in such a sweet nothingness is not a sustainable state. As mentioned previously, I have heard statements when one says that they need to find their other half to be complete. I am rather up for those who believe that two full must find each other and create balance where both can flourish and grow.

Put simply, above all else, love fearlessly.

No.Sex

I had a dull day and stared at my laptop screen, reading the Google landing page title like hundred times. I was not distracted or in a funny mood, just had one of those moments when I wanted to do exactly nothing. As I rested my eyes on that screen, my fingers started to run on the keyboard and typed in a question which came to my mind.
Superlatives.
The most searched words / topics
The result of this micro improvised exploration turned out not too dazzling... Here it runs, with the top 10 list of humanly conversed topics:
Adult Content – approx. 548 million/each year
Weather – 405 million/each year
Celebrities – 86 million/each year
Shopping – 56 million/each year
Lottery – 30 million/each year
Sports
Consumer technology
News
Movies
Beauty

We blather about sex, generalities, success and glam, purchases, technology and all related to entertainment and our appearance.
It resembles that people are occupied by wanting to

be liked, feel good, look good, get nice things, treat themselves well, be important to one or to some.

I wanted to cover a topic which is interesting to all and where you will tilt your head up and say hey, I must read this.

So, I picked sex out of all. I feel that it's a very overexposed but under-discussed topic.

I made this our little chapter no.Sex.

This is probably the chapter which got rewritten the most. It had the conservative shy version, the naive dreamer version, the crazy steamy curious version, the passionate experimental version and so many more... It is also the one which caused me the most sleepless nights as I was thinking what I can throw on paper and how much weight those pages could carry. I had those flaming face moments which very often turned into hours and days. I felt so damn embarrassed to even think back or recall some old shared and heard stories and memories. Yet, I have learned to love these words and sentences and slowly this chapter became one of my very favourite one.

So, let me get started. I leave you to decide which version, I have left in the final printed book.

`In need of intimacy, why would you abuse someone if you can help yourself? ` This was a sentence from my friend. She dropped it in the middle of a semi-formal dinner with some of our newly met friends. Imagine the shocked silence and then the burst of the biggest laugh. The topic was juicier than the steak on the dinner plate. We have carried on discussing a full spectrum of toys for self-entertainment. Never heard of gadgets and tools.

Opposed to the first moment of embarrassment, we seemed to know much more about this topic than I have expected.

We all have agreed, that one should not go for a one-night stand if the play-rules are not lined up. The other party must be clear on the intention and not to be left with any hopes for more than what the encounter is.

And naturally, if you can't do it without emotional attachments, hurt or shame, then better to take a walk in the `candy shop` and help yourself.

Sex and love are like a mix and match at the Victoria Secret Valentine's day sale...

What's chemistry? Why we are attracted suddenly when we had amazing sex?

`The feel of your touch, the softness of skin on skin, the sweet long talks, your deep voice, dark sparkly eyes, the ecstasy of lightly biting lips, the warmth of your breath on my cheeks and neck, the electric strike on the spine from adrenalin meeting passion, pull into a doorstep to endlessly kiss, a spin in your arms to lose all realistic senses.`

`I softly kiss your lip. You grab my hands and pull me close. Now your tongue enters my mouth and our eyes shut to together enter a different zone. You hold my waste and slide your hands to grab me good, into my flash, with passion. My hands are running down on your spine and then up again to pull you by under your shoulders. I quickly rip your T-shirt off. I am so comfy in our zone that I can't open my eyes, but I want to see your body. And need to see that new tattoo, so excited to see it! Open eyes, staring at you for a second to admire the sight and I start gently biting you. Yes, every inch of your gorgeous skin, lower, lower, lower on your chest, lower, lower, lower. When I reach at waistline, you undress me with one quick move. You pick me up. Now my legs wrapped around your waist. We spin and turn and laugh how we bounce into all the things in the room. Just as we find the bed, you are immediately striking in and we are possibly the closest to each other. Deep and fast. Great rhythm. Like dancing with our waists. Back to our zone. Where only the two can enter. And it is all for us. Pure. Pleasure. Fun. Never enough of each other's touch moments. Then you lay next to me and I feel every of your breath, falling asleep slowly. Your fingers running tiny circles around the last tip of my fingers. Soft and teasing. Our hands slide slowly and lock together. We dream the same dream when suddenly it is us...stop time for those rare moments-when everything just feels natural and at its purest and you just levitate in splendour. `

These little snaps of a heated meet could symbolize the stirring stages when two passionate individuals find each other floating on the same wavelength. And then great sex happens. But is it only a bodily experience? Could that be only that much?

People are people, we are no different, we just fall in love with the person who gives us what we want at that moment. We are led by emotions and emotions breed from actions and its interpretation. Therefore, we feel in love just after we had amazing sex.

Sex can be just a physical act. Some can do it randomly and casually. Cabotage. But it is never just as that. Sex is 90% mental. If it's about curiosity and the drive for doing, then you won't get pleasure.

Have you ever met someone, a stranger or a friend of a friend, who you could instantly tell was authentic, happy, settled— and absolutely magnetic? Have you ever wondered, what's their secret? Why don't I feel the same way?

Those able to reawaken that magnetic power are able to shift their self-loathing habits into self-loving habits. The late legendary intimacy expert and author of Tantra Touch, Psalm Isadora, helped tens of thousands of people release their shame on this topic, re-joy and access their true divine self through sexual healing.

The Whole World is starving for Sexual Healing. It is not just a Marvin Gaye song. Our sexual energy is the connection between body and soul, between us and others. Our sexuality holds the answer to our fears, traumas, those feelings of disconnection. Sexual healing can empower us to know ourselves, our partner and the surrounding world better. Used carefully, this is an enormous source of abundant energy. It can help you to reconnect with yourself when lost between physical places and countries.

As Isadora said in an interesting podcast interview *'Sexual Energy is this powerful, creative force inside of us that manifests and creates our entire life. Sex isn't just about having sex. It's about how we express ourselves, or manifest possibilities. Any body-shame or unhealthy sexual beliefs and behaviour will end up affecting your self-esteem, relationships and career. Our society tells us that sex is dirty and sinful — but we're all birthed from sex to experience the fullness of life. If you can release your sexual energy to good use, you'll live more authentically, your intuition will be better, and you'll open yourself up to enjoying all the pleasures of life.* `Take her idea with a pinch of salt and go turn your sexual energy into something productive and settling.

With all honesty, we know that if your sexual life is set up in a satisfying way, having no worries and conflicting thoughts there, then you will feel lighter and more comforted than any other aspects of your life would have an impact on how you hold up getting through your days.
Reaching this settling feeling has more importance when home becomes a foreign expression, and everything is stirring around you. Do not be shy to deal with this topic as dearly as you focus on other matters when relocating.
Use your sexual energy happily and wise when crosscountries!

Drip-Drops

Relocate with your partner; decide how to manage a new relationship when moving away at an early stage; find new love at your new place and move again together; any of these scenarios are probing yet there are great ways to lead a satisfying and happy relationship being distant or together in the afresh. Have your game-plan laid. Main suggestion for all times: transparency is key in any relationship!

Two full must find each other and create balance where both can flourish and grow.

Turn your energy into that relationship what you have signed up for. Feed it, nurture it and as you do, also work on yourself to be the best partner you can be.

Make love!

Turn your sexual energy into something really satisfying!

Keep going, stay abroad

Motivation

You need to stay motivated to stay abroad and establish a comfortable life, living anywhere. Else by the first remora you will fleet.
Is it really motivation what you need?
How far and how long one can go when having a great goal in mind?
Is it the mind which need to hold the necessary willpower to stay abroad and keep going?

Just think of a moment when someone compliments or teases you. Not just anyone but add that it's a person you respect, look up to and admire. That flash of adrenalin. That sudden warmth rushing through your veins and blushing you from head to toe. Like the first days when you have moved abroad, and you are discovering the pleasant new. I always wanted to preserve this early hype and promised myself that I stay curious and, on the discovery, to indulge in the little pleasantries of my newly chosen home.
However as easy as it sounds; it is a hell of a grind to stay there. And I did not manage without exception. I see it as a downtime to give me one or more realizations and help me to make changes for my later benefit. I am throwing this on paper with a total retrospect and keeping it in mind that in the exact moment, I had no idea why I was feeling disturbed, uncomfortable, restless and many more displeasing emotions. So, firstly, be patient and do not look for

an instant answer. It's part of the discoveries.

Ten years back, I lived in London, on the North-East side, closed to a DLR station called Angels. I wonder why this name when the place had nothing to do with Heaven or anything close to where Angels would stay. Often, I thought of the opposite implication. For instance, when I was chased for my purse by a bunch of teenage boys on rainy winter nights, while walking home. That's not the scene which matter the most but the sensation, I have arrived to after a year and a half spent in this lovely city. Professionally, I liked my hotel job, yet I felt that I was ready to do more. Outside of work, I was desperate. Desperate to leave the noise, the crowd, the thieves, the beggars, the dirt, the hours on crammed public transport or the long walks in the rain, when I could not afford to top up my Oyster card. I could not help but feel anger when I looked out on the window and it was a dark hazy day and I knew that I had an hour walk to get to work with few possible hold-ups on my way. Then the same on my return. My home meant a 1.5 by 2.2 meters whole in the wall, shared bathroom with five or occasionally more flat mates and a tiny airless kitchen where everything mysteriously evaporates from the fridge. Not that you would be able to buy lots of fresh products or enjoy some great meals on an ordinary low budget. No wonder, I spent most of my time in the gym, walking the parks or the river bench or trying to see some friends when our schedule would meet. But, man, I got exhausted of this lifestyle! I do love London, as a tourist. For maximum four, five days, that's my mental limit. Living there was, certainly not my `cup of tea`. I could catch myself in a mental survival mode. I had to consciously control every breath and thought and forcingly find a momentary solution to each negative vibe that would leave my body. You can fit in many places, but it doesn't mean you belong there.

`It's never difficult to be right when you are alone. ` - credit to Esther Perel. No sweat. I could have accepted those firstly unpleasant feelings, adopted and lived on with them. But I knew that I can't let these feelings overwhelm me and change me into a grinch, so I started to plan for my exit. I turned my focus to what I wish to have in my days rather than fighting what was evident and existent in my current reality. I draw a brainy picture and literally lived for it. Within two weeks or so, a call arrived to me and I got a second opportunity to get to Malta. Since it was not my first chance to relocate there, I took it as a sign that I have some agenda on this tiny Mediterranean island. On a lucky Friday the 13th, I landed in Malta and my mood was instantly changed to sunny just like the weather.

The other deal breaker arrived to me on Salt island, one of the groups of `green capes`, a windy paradise-pictured place in the middle of the ocean, just a few hundred kilometres off the Senegal coast. I thought, I knew what a tropical place can be and felt confident that it will be truly bliss on Earth. I had a night flight and landed in complete darkness. I could have been suspicious for not seeing any lights down under, but the first excitement overwrote this minor detail. And brother, how lucky I was to have arrived in the night! Otherwise, I might have taken the first flight back.

This patch of a tropical island was a flat desert, you could see from one edge to the other if there was a stop on the constant sandstorm, leaving us with dusky sights. With waives curving back at two meters tops, allowing only the brave one to swim and the kite lovers to have fun. With tiny market-stalls which gets topped up when the boat reached over the strong currents from the other, but green islands. The supermarket where if there was yogurt or toilet paper, the news was spreading as wild-fire and all dropped our work to run to the shop. There were few deal-breaker places, I have lived at, yet this looked to be the most troublesome so far. Here, most commodities lacked, more necessities were not available while naturally, basic civilizational comforts were not known. The purity of the locals made up for a lot, I must admit. I felt like the first day in the gym. You hurt everywhere and consciously, you feel pain at corporal places, you never knew existed on your body, yet in the hope of distant improvement, you go for every session. The struggles are milder, and your frame now can take heavier loads. You feel ease and to get on, becomes natural. That's a gym success story. Unfortunately? - not mine for CV.

I fought it and told myself to stay put, it will get better. I lifted my mood with sports and gathered great, amazingly charming new friends. I loved them to bits and blessed the time spent with them. It was not enough to kill my inner call for an escape. I was in the tropics. On a tiny, deserted island. As I always imagined how my life should evolve. But this was not that island. Surely, too deserted, and way too much of nothing I could get a grip on to take a liking on Sal.

Not to mention my professional disappointment, that totally hindered me back. I was where I have left off, few years earlier. Back to a flat day and night struggle for no advancement. And I refused to stay in my resort manager job in the Seychelles for just this? I was disappointed in myself. I could have done with better judgement to see where the promises, and where real probability laid. Much better. But, it was my decision at the end, so had to try to settle with it, at least for a while. Till my mission was complete for which I gave my word to. Till the moment came to fulfil the promises and see if really there would be a shot for my next appointment. I owned it to myself and to my overly enthusiastic team. I have never met with a group of young professionals who would hold such a genuine and burning passion. And my Assistant. I was so darn lucky to work with him. The best guy ever. We had such an expertly chemistry, him holding all the virtues, I don't have and vice versa. We could have built the 8th Wonder of the World! We were hungry to learn and succeed with all our difficulties along the path. I have great affection to them. And, to my Boss, with whom I had a few years of coworking history, and I could feel that he was also not in the place where he would have wanted to be. He struggled to hold the team down and together along with all the corporate and construction issues he was haphazardly de-tangling. The atmosphere was tense. Yet we were rowing the boat, paddling for survival in the sea of uncertainties. This works for a while. Absolutely. Even worth all the effort if it is for a final goal. We had nothing on the horizon though. The pictures, I have painted on the sky for my guys to look at, were fading away as the pledges given to me earlier were confirmed to be only promises.

The solution came in a form, I would have never wished for. Nevertheless, it was one.

I got sick. We had a daily routine to handle stomach flues as the food situation was somewhat challenging, yet my flue did not have an intention to go away. After weeks of not eating or drinking, with limited medical assistance, I have decided to pull a preventive evacuation and fly home to get a proper diagnose and treatment. I was consent nauseous and lost like 10 kilograms weight by the time, I have reached the department of tropical diseases in my home country. They showed a parasite and two bacteria in my stomach and in the small intestines. They cosily spread and started to weaken the walls and functions of those organs. I underwent an intense care treatment with drips, shots and what not. Started to test liquids and fluid food. I was adamant and pushed my moral. I had a call to let the team fly with more trained wings and succeed. They deserve it, they earned the best chance. After a month, I returned to the island for a second round, did what I have agreed to, left the team strongly prepared as solid as we could achieve in an eyeblink of time and with the last kick from my executive, left the place for good. To save me. Not for the escape. Still my departure served as both. It took me two years to be able to eat solid and various food again and still the recovery is ongoing as most likely I will carry some repercussions for a lifetime.

I always wanted to make everyone better. It was my deepest motivation to see the ones, who showed determination, succeed. Efforted to help and be resourceful and guide and hold up the people I have worked with and had around as friends. I kept giving and providing mentally, spiritually, physically and financially. And to feed my own soul, I was walking towards my own dream. At least that's what I was telling myself. I kept choosing the wrong path where there was no glory just sweat. Where I crossed unappreciative and abusive people. But I loved them. Loved them and worked even harder when pushed back. I didn't get closer to my dream. Or maybe. It can be just a detour. I might find out later. `Your end goal may change along the way, but you will never know unless you get going. `- as Daymond John says. Nevertheless, I have travelled to dreamy places and distracted me with a mirage on the horizon. I might not become the best VP, might not get the chance to be a partner, a mother, a private island resort owner. My inspiration can change and will continuously. It evolves as I grow through experiences and under pressures. I stay moving with new ideas to conquer. Call it motivation, call it a dream, call it a desire, call it a goal, call it a move, call it a call. It does not matter how you name it. It is not necessarily an end to a journey and not a mental state or physical place to reach. You can stay put or you can get going, it is absolutely your choice.

I am happy and grateful. For being able to share and give. For concluding this book. I had this on my chest for years and it feels amazing to have done it. The result was not my motivation. The work was. Voila!

I was once thinking to create a website to make people happy every day. This would have been one of

the micro-projects, I wished to run when I was seeing ever-various personal and professional burdens holding top scorers and other teammates back.
The idea ran as this; it could be a fun page with nice and motivational content. But wait a second! How would you ever know what motivates people? What makes them feel well, what resonates with their current mindset and heart-set?
As we wake every morning and walk through the day to then retire to bed and leave this circle behind, we must realise that we do change at least a dozen times. So how a generic approach would serve everyone? Impossible. And I do not think that this word exists, even yet I'm writing it down. We do feel uplifted by the things we momentarily resonate with. We focus and give attention to those impulses which are corresponding to our thinking and feelings in the flowing second.

Exercise - do this with your buddy:
Look around the room and spot five things in red colour!
Close your eyes and list 5 things that are blue in the room?! Did you get any scores?
Why did I ask for the blue items when firstly I wanted you to observe the red ones?
Exactly to show you how selective our focus is, how we can be misled by external drivers and due to that, how we often miss to see rational facts and opportunities.
There is a ton of information surrounding us and it is humanly not possible to absorb every little thing. You would not use your energy to notice certain things unless it serves your thought, purpose or feeds on

your emotions. You can filter and sharpen your focus around and towards anything if you make a conscious choice to do so. This is all of what you need, to keep going.
You need your own triggers to stay motivated. Whether as simple as getting up in the morning and getting to your work on time or as hefty as becoming the next Tony Robbins, we all need lighthouses to keep the eyes on, when navigating on the seven-sees. For this- and few other various reasons – my motivational website did not happen.

Ok, so you need triggers. Sounds simple and easy. Why it doesn't work so smoothly in the daily practise then? What other tricks can you use to get ahead in a direction pleasing to you?
Mel Robbins has developed a great idea around this topic. She calls it The 5 Second Rule. I really do admire that woman, especially how she passionately explains her story of finding her solution to stay in the game and go for her goals. She has lost her job; her husband has failed their family businesses and their house was going under the hammer due to the delayed mortgage payments. She has piled up a lot of crap as excuses, not to do what she has known that must be done. She could have walked out of her door and sorted her things but instead it was easier to stay in bed and feel sorry for herself. She has accepted those obstacles and made them hard-rock facts to justify how it cannot be done. Meanwhile her family life and marriage were slowly going shipwrecked.
We all have a tendency to sink into our excuses and try buying time with thoughts like I will do it, when I will be more fit, when I will be promoted, when I will

be married, when I move house, when my hair grows...pfft all these are time wasters, big time ... She has listened to lots of smart people and advises, went to therapy even and every evening, she folded her head in bed, with a great motivation that next morning, she will wake up with the alarm, jump out of bed and change all around. 7 am the next morning, alarm goes off...she opens her eyes to stare at the ceiling and in less than half a minute hits the snooze. The snooze turns into a few more hours of sleep. What happened there? Where is her burning motivation? It was gone with that 25 seconds where she overthought her day and the list of to-does and her conscious has decided that her agenda is rather a challenge then a walk in the park and made her hit that snooze to sleep in. She had days passing the same way. One gloomy cold morning, as fast as she opened her eyes, with the same instant move, she sprang out of bed. And since then, she has been unstoppable. What happened there? Where is her stubborn conscious, sending alerts and keeping her in bed? Well, as she explains, motivation is rubbish. Your brain has an automatic response to stop you from what seems a potential threat. Also, in a tiny moment, the emotions can come in and make you feel like you don't want, or you can't do it anymore. You need to learn how to take control in a micro moment and silence the hesitation! That's a decision. Ignore that tiny moment when your brain tries to sabotage you, decide and start!

Here's a one-liner definition of The 5 Second Rule: If you have an impulse to act on a goal, you must physically move within 5 seconds or your brain will kill the idea.

Why would you put anything on hold?
You find the way, or the way finds you!
This thought came to my mind because of my knee
pain. On a Saturday night, I was sitting on my couch
and hesitated; should I wait to run the Malta
Marathon till I'm well trained, till I have no injury or
pain, shall I put everything on hold around me only
because I run a bit on a sunny Sunday? No. The body
achieves what the mind decides.
`Life is what you make it`-as Eleanor Roosevelt said it
very well.
The French say that all good things come in small
portions. Mainly that is for their cuisine. However, I
believe that the Universe measures and gives us small
drops, small portions of the great things at times as
an impulse to drag you back on your path or direct
you. If we are in the moment and ready to sense it, it
can be a delight. A real delight and a pointer for
what's next. Our past can be a source of motivation.

At times, in the beginning of new projects or
perspectives, you may only have hopes and dreams
but as long as you have faith and strength to believe
in it and you work for them, you will succeed!
Energise yourself and everyone around you. People
would listen just about anything if it gives them hope,
make them feel better or justifies their current
behaviour or thought process. We are drawn to
anything that resonates with current thoughts,
justify, verify, amplify, reassures our decisions, makes
us feel better, generates the emotions we are seeking
and keeps us on the go with results and more hope.

We all have a passion point, a trigger, something that can drive us. You must translate the simple tasks. Make them exciting obstacles. Describe them in your spoken language, with words which bring out the best action from you. Scale it all, to your drive! Meaningful triggers create an emotion which is in your subconscious and your strongest drive. The goal or goals must be very precise, you need to decide why you want what you just dreamed up and what it will give you in your life and inner World.
Fills a need? Fills a gap? Enhances existing circumstances? Adds a new aspect? Excites a new perspective? Invites a new lifestyle, habits, knowledge or skill? Entertains?
We could go on with a long list. You name it as you wish. If it makes you jump for it, it is a great trigger! That is the only measure.
Triggers are absolutely subjective and not objective. One is not suitable for everyone, but one is suitable for every one.
Let me give you an example to prove this suggestion. Buying a flight ticket is not exactly a defined trigger. The feeling you feel - being some heartbeat in your chest, the hype in your head a little shake in your whole body - when you imagine yourself arriving at your destination and seeing the first sight. That will be a cool picture to paint in your mind and a pretty decent and strong trigger.
Good emotionally nested triggers make you eager to run for them. You must phrase, think and picture your goals in a most sensational way to move the most of your senses and impact your emotions.
Write it down. Handwritten! So, your brain gets it and it sinks in your subconscious mind. I like to hang

stickers around me with my key words, usually on the inside of the entrance door, on my work desk, on my laptop case, on my phone cover, on my coffee machine and so on, to keep myself reminded. As the next step, you must be certain that you reach whatever you have pictured.

Do not be scared if you do not have the ways and means yet but be always totally sure of summoning it. Do not question or `if` it! Believe. Try one, two, every way, when you think that you ran out of ways, study and find even more. Keep stretching yourself. Use your emotional triggers, you wrote down at the beginning and make yourself jump for it, again and again!

How many times have you flipped, and blind pointed on the World map? How many times you have written a country list and relisted the rankings after each advising conversation you have had with friends or relatives? I did and still do many times with my best friend! However, during my past professional expat years and countries - still counting! -, I have figured that the map flipping method might not be the best and easiest way to relocate my life. It is certainly a huge adrenalin boosted adventure, yet it can turn out to be more struggle and less fun in proportion.

I have learned through experience and from wise and relocation-seasoned friends that really all coins have two sides. We explore, observe, sense and learn by sharing, get inspired to pass on our practicalities and it should all be like a circle and a chain reaction.

I have been riding the rollercoaster between countries for a while and when hitting the down strip,

only a nice reset would have helped me to stay put and do not buy a ticket home - or to a sweet tropical destination. My lasting motivation hacks are working for me, they do because I have exploited many ways to shake myself up and established a good speed of recovery after a fall. It depends on your strategies and their effectiveness how fast you get up. What you really should play with is your sales mastery - AKA how to sell again and again to yourself!?
Once a trigger gets exhausted, it can have less impact on your emotions hence the response will be much lower too.

Easing place. Meditate. In every hometown, I usually had my favourite spot. A place which was dear to my eyes, my heart and mostly uplifted my spirit with its sight, energy, vibes, sounds, smells or any more sensory aspects. It would shift my focus, purify my mind and let me turn my attention back on the important.
I would retire to sit on the staircase of the Sacre Coeur in Paris and watch the flow of happy and curious tourist along with those extremely talented street artists. I would get inspired by their enthusiasm and figure new trigger words and impacts to continue with my agenda.
In Malta, it was the Dingli Cliffs. When something hurts, I ran off to sit on the cliffs. Preferably at sunset. It was the most dramatic and Earth shaking when the weather was a bit rainy. The reflection of the clouds would play hide and seek on the mirror flat open ocean while close to the shore, the waives would loudly splash the coast and nearly catch the top of the 250 meters high cliffs. I have gathered

strength from those rough natural vibes and enjoyed the show of all elements.

This is a game of focus. Concentrate to stay in the now before your conscious rouse and stops you in the fly. Go for the words which are formed in your mind due to your current feelings. Make note of these and review them few or more times to select your favourites.

You can make micro-changes in regards of your triggers, do not worry, when you apply them in enough key areas, they will make a compound result and lead you to an impactful outcome. One which fulfils you. And makes you stick.

Listen. Do not just hear what you want to hear. Listen as it can be a great source of information. Information which can be translated into new knowledge. And knowledge is a great drive. You discover new topics to dive into and you find yourself while submerging in it.

We often make the mistake to get into conversations with a pre-directed agenda. Recurrently, I catch guest doing this! They know what they will say and push with what I want to or not want to hear. They must be practising a pitch even rehearsing it in their head before getting to the chat. Is that right? Do you recall yourself doing that? They already know what they want as the conclusion. They use the plot to display one or more of their brilliant conversation skills and get to what they deem as a great persuasion when you leave with the exact same thoughts what you have started off. The issue is that this is a session of zero communication.

Please start listening. Do not let your mind wander

around and just wait for your time to talk. Do not divert and start thinking about what your answer will be when it is your turn. Do not bark out prefabricated sentences with no respect of the conversing partner. Trust me, you do not need to have an answer in a dialogue. It is a dialogue to exchange ideas and see each other's perspectives. There is no written rule that you must walk away with a finished chapter and with one straight closure.

If I have explained what a monologue was, you get a better take on this. So, when you are in your head. You are thinking. Let's say 80% of our awake time, we tend to do so. It is a run of ideas, opinions, pictures attached to your feelings and to the current context you are in. You go to the shopping centre and walk at that pretty handcraft shop you love. Your mind is registering all the items you see and you start construction a monologue, do I have to buy something for my paint project, did I miss that rosewood brown colour of oil paint and if I have added more of sunset red, would that look terrific? The picture I have seen over there had that colour applied, let me go back to that isle and check? Oh yeah, like it like it, shall I buy it then? I don't need a whole tube...or I borrow some from my friend who must have the same! She has, as she was painting those cute kids' room wall pieces and showed me all the colours she has bought. Maybe I just call her and ask, better to call. And I dial her number. This is a monologue. No pre-written agenda, just a flow of ideas and internal exchange, fed from your own toolbox.

You do not think and have a monologue to conquest. You are listening to your inner self and like a software colliding, reviewing facts and information. You are creating your thoughts and emotions like that. You will not place the dot to the end of your thought with a previously used cliché, but you will still go through it and let new impulses come in and strive to come to a desired outcome. I would not suppose that you aim at a full solution. Because the solution will come from the execution eventually.

It is similar in a dialogue, where you suppose to run that information with another collaborating head and not in your own. You have the luxury to use the other's toolboxes and mesh up incredible new impulses to inspire you. You may find new ways and solutions. You might get cool friends. But surely, you will leave the conversation more energised than ever!

I have an extra tip here; if you can, please do use your language skills. Speaking a foreign language will allow your mind to switch to a new gear and start to understand things which you did not even think of previously. It is a new insight. It opens a new alley in your mind so that you are thinking in a new perspective and filter things through a concept of that other language.

Muse. Can be a person or things. You may spend time with a person who simply is so charismatic and uplifting that you can't help but get really charged when being around. A person who is constantly doing and creating and injects the same motives in you just be standing next to them.

You may choose an object, a thing as your Muse. If this sounds a little tricky, let me give you some examples here. I have many friends with their lucky charms. They have a bracelet, a necklace, an old Teddy bear which they firmly believe that has special powers. It has their happy vibes locked in them and they do pass it on. Always ready when needed. Very conveniently, they just get this object around them and it is enough of an inspiration to lift them emotionally and eventually lead them to a reset.

Always, the answer is in front of you. You can develop a question and your own method, which will unlock the answer and lead you to the desired trigger. Keep going.

People started to gather on the edge of the cliffs as the watchman in the lighthouse would do, when he sees a sudden rise of the sea. There was a surge, a big storm forming, bigger than you have ever seen or heard of. The sea raised to the height of a skyscraper and the waves became unrecognisable in the whole whirlwinds of the seas. When everyone thought that it will be a tsunami and the city will be washed away in seconds, a man raised from the water. He casually walked with his surfboard and switched off the huge 4D projector behind him.
What? This is awkward. You bit off your nails for this light ending?
Why am I telling you this story? Everyone likes the nerve wrecking stories where you bite your lips to finally reach the peak and get your big bang cumulation. It is a complete nonsense though. But it's dramatic, it's entertaining and it perfectly sets the scene for our next topic. Expectations.

Expectations

I often thought that the Universe lost my address, or I am moving too much and too fast for the Universe to find me...I had my portion of wishes, longings and expectations. But there is no such a thing what we deserve. We are all in the same oyster and the shell withholds events which we chose to live or not to participate. But we have the choice. We observe and endure it all through our own perception.

It is what it is. We should not go in with anticipation, especially when relocating to the unknown. Expectations destroy the experience and won't let you see things how they are. You will only focus on the things you have pre-pictured in your mind and keenly search for those details; which if they are not found, there you go, disappointment ready, steady, served!

Someone can tell you that something is really good. Then you carefully follow the advice and repeat the same things, just to conclude, that you do not like it at all.

Why is that exactly? It is the indirect result of your expectation. Which is an infusion between the clues you have received from the storyteller – those highlights they have picked according to their taste - and your own exposures mixed with your previous actuality and all whose have shaped your lens of perception. The pre-idea is shaped, and the mood is set by what you have heard. Yet, your feelings will not be exactly what your adviser had lived through. This projection is yours now, but with the high expectation of the same fun outcome as your storyteller had told you. It will not necessarily match up and then will cause disappointment. For that and some other reasons, I would rather not waste time to build up ideas. By all means, I take a suggestion and often decide to go for the same discussed things, but I refrain from running my mind to paint the episode beforehand. I prefer to enjoy without looking out for preconditioned details. I wish to pick my own moments and highlights, live them through, and make up my memories from the experience.

Do you like surprises? If you would know everything in advance, would you be able to experience those magical moments when something pleasant just crops up totally unexpected? Like when I was walking around on the top of the TV tower in Prague and seemed to pass my Brazilian friend's husband for two times. He looked familiar but I have dashed away the idea as they have moved back home years ago, from London where we have worked together. But then he suddenly jumped on my neck, hugged me and started screaming down at his wife, look who is here, look, you won't believe it. I turned my face and saw my friend. With the same move, swung around and climbed the stairs with wind-speed to reach her. Would I have ever expected to spend a few days with them in Prague when I have already moved to Malta and they were back in Brazil for years? We lost contact and yet, here we were. In Prague, meeting by chance.
I know that it's an extreme, but would you destroy the happiness of first discoveries, the surprise of the new impressions, the encounters of the unrepeatable

and mainly, the crash with adorable friends?
I fully know that relocating your life is not
comparable to a walk in the park when surprises are
welcome. Yet, I suggest that you follow a very
minimal cushioning prep to settle your conscious and
let the wonderful details land at their place!

I think of some locations, I ended up living and I
wonder how I have managed. How we have
managed? I mean, between my colleagues, we were
mostly European nations, used to comfort and all
what civilization can offer. We were accustomed to
run to the shop and find whatever we desire and
have all facilities to entertain our desires or live for
our hobbies in our free time. Opposed to the not
even comparable environments, we found ourselves
in. At some locations, even clean water was an issue.
And food. We were happy to eat. Just like that.
Remote locations are an extra challenge to
relocation. You will never have your usual or at least
similar commodities than home... Not even things to
satisfy basic human needs. Yes, as I have previously
mentioned for the Cape Verdes, I had a strong
expectation of finding a tropical paradise, the
cumulation of all my daydreams. Even worse, I admit,
I took an assumption that it will be THE place for me.
This destination was all the unimaginable.

But how do we adapt in such places? And why would
we take on a ruffle like that?
What is the most difficult when living in a very
remote location?
What do we miss the most?

How can we turn the lacking into fulfilment?

When we move, or our life circumstances are changing, we make a mistake to still search for the same usual things. We need to let go and start anew. Do not take your or other advisers` ideas of any place for granted.
There is no need to adapt in a strict meaning, when you are ready to start as a blank page.
I do not say, not to have ambitions and goals. That's exactly the opposite, I am suggesting. You must have a strong idea on your why to be where you are and what you wish to achieve with your stay, however, try not to build too much of the pretty details on the how in advance.
It makes a new place most difficulty liveable and enjoyable if we are preoccupied with our pre-assumptions and keenly look for the same items we had at home or strictly fixated what we have imagined that we will have at the picked location.
We miss the things and commodities most what we assume to be fundamentals for our life. I can tell you that nothing is indispensable - apart from the life-threatening essentials such as water and clean food supply – everything else is just what we place in our sharp focus to be a must. I am not a hippie and would not suggest leaving a greatly simple life or to eliminate all the luxuries or conveniences.
It is a mind-shift, an approach what I imply here; that you learn to value what is available and abundant. Replace the usual non- findable with the new available. Allow the rest of your common items and settings to become the extra and disposable. Turn the lacking into fulfilment, see the glass half full and

stay on the lookout for all the unique goodies at every place you visit or settle at.

For instance, moving to Orlando was a great choice still I had this picture in my head that I would be going around, visiting places and I will be mobile on my own as everywhere else so far. When reaching there, I had to realise that distances between localities in Florida are great and public transport is nearly non-existent. I was stuck at my house and unable to reach any place on foot. The closest park or supermarket were some 5 miles away along the highway. I needed a car if I did not want to depend on others. Surely, I felt let-down. I could have looked around and gathered the beauty of the resort where I have stayed, the amazingly pleasant colleagues and fun team I was surrounded with, the swimming pool in front of my nose and the gym next to my office. Instead, I was occupied with a pressing fact to purchase a car as soon as possible. This single thought took over for weeks and made me loose the chance to enjoy the plenty positives offered by my new home.

It's just one of my short fables on how expectations build up and can taint your vision from seeing clear. It eats up your time from fun. I personally find it very powerful to learn and gain strength from our experiences. Here are mine, shared generously, so, you don't need to play your precious trials.

The heavy stuff: Fear, hesitation, giving up

I do not like negative talk. If you have noticed, I purposely avoided any resistive or non-affirmative matters. It is not because I letitate and think that life is only about good but simply because it is more pleasant to stay on the bright side. We have enough to deal with in the everyday encounters. And because I want you to start thinking and living in this frame. The more we are, the better this World becomes and the less nonsense BS we will need to face.

I just mentioned a word, letitate. It is not a typo. Do you recall what it means?

It is a word to summarise all the let it boosting prompts, you can possibly squeeze into one simple expression; let it be, let it go, let it change you, let it break you, let it build you, let it lead you, let it be explored...add anything that may give you the kick you need.

The emotional hurdles of a relocation. Clearly, they are the ones to make you turn back and give in. You follow instructions, you prepare, and you think that you are ready and when you get there, s**t hits the fan and you realise that you are not ready at all. Your mind, spirit and soul emotionally can't be ready because we are human, and all humans are reliant on habits, routines and communities. We live by our patterns and when all gets out of place, it becomes a burden to just get through the days.

Your head and heart are still behind but your body lives there now...

In retrospect, some of my stories seem little and insignificant. Being there and living it through was a totally different game though. In Paris for instance, I had passed plenty sleepless nights until I have figured a self-built safety device. My apartment was on the

174

ground floor with a full size, double winged door and two tall French windows. Practically, you could have walked in without even realising that you are not using the entrance. The flat was facing a garden, yet it was not the most assuring for me to sleep with such open entries around my façade. I felt strong fear every day as the night had fallen. I have questioned hundred times, why am I here and why I have accepted this housing? It was really stretching my nerves and as I was getting less and less sleep, I was building up more and more resistance against my new location. I slowly started to doubt the aspects which I firstly enjoyed and liked. I took a full turn and fear had dragged me into the bush. Every night was a battle and each morning a release. The solution came from the same head which has built up all the nonsense struggles. As a fact, I have pushed some heavy furniture to the tall doors and requested shutters on the windows. I have played my mind. I won over me.

One night, back in Mahe, the roof of the hotel set on fire. As the one in charge, I was called in and until the fire fighters had arrived, we got in action to hold back the flames. While standing up there, with the water hose in my hands, I felt strong fear, as at this time, I feared the uncontrollable, which made the situation even worse. I battled between my thoughts and asked myself if I had gone insane for staying here, on the roof at that moment. I have questioned if I had taken the best possible route and if I shall give up this hectic lifestyle for something more predictable and less risky. For long moments, I could not control my head, at times my mind was playing games at me and at the other extreme, my body was shaking in horror.

`Evacuate or stay put and don't create commotion or worst, a panic!?`I have asked myself multiplied times. In any similar situation, I could have passed on my jitters to others, only to ease my angst, but I had no luxury of such. I was the one, everyone looked at, for the settling solution and to dismantle the built-up tensions. So, I took a deep breath, collected all my remaining courage and decided to look only at a minute at a time. I forcefully have blocked the chatter in my head and stayed looking at the bare happenings. And the fire was finally extinguished in just less than a half an hour, without any guest noticing it. It rather felt hours. This time proved to be a real deal breaker. I was never so close to quit. It is to the credit of the few great friends who held my hand from far and some people on the island. Their support was incredible to talk this encounter through and it surely safeguarded my sanity. And it kept me going. Anchored me. I thank them today, to make me stay in this amazing place.

Life is really beautiful if you allow yourself to live it. Of course, you pass through moments, hours and days when you see everything dark. Your horse-blinders get stuck on your face and you fail to turn your head and shake it off. But hey, don't sit and sob actionless, sealed off from all the good out there. Take your lessons and continue.

Fear is heavy to handle just as hesitation; they both must be held on a short leash. As we have said in the previous chapters, we all tend to procrastinate and rather `wait until it is the right time'. I do it when I finished school, when I learnt that language, when I get fitter, when my hair is longer etc.... when when

when when all conditioning and a waste!
Stop waiting! Stop your hesitation and stop buying time for the day when ..., being anxious and unhappy to then reach THE DAY when you should finally be joyful, and you do not even know what you were so excited waiting for. Be cheerful until you wake up every morning. Healthy and strong and capable of doing anything. Tomorrow might not come one day...would you like to waste more time till you get to your perfect? Or accept that you need no perfection to be happy. All the trips and falls and misconceptions which are holding you back, are time stealers.

Sometimes we become comfortably uncomfortable, accepting our self-defeating thought patterns as part of life. By realizing you have something to give to your friends, your community and yourself, you can turn that pain inside of you into purposeful drive. Wherever you decide to bring your light, you'll shine ten times brighter for all of the darkness you've encountered.

Remember, that you see the same sight, your feeling depends where you focus on the bright or the dark side, inside or outside.

The way forward is ahead not backwards.

Maybe lucky, but I never had time for stumbling or over thinking. I had to pick the learning and move on to the next thing. This helped me not to fall into depression or not to feel bad about failings. Of course, I had those moments when my body would shake from tiredness and my eyes got teary for losing out on making another perfect stride.

I have forced my brain to take over and moved forward. In those moments, I focused to stay sober

and reasonable. Strictly analysed the scenario and got the pluses and minuses. Accepted my previous choices. Took all the conclusions. Then left the rest behind.
What you are moving towards is moving towards you!
Do me a favour. Ok, not for me. For you! Overcome your pitying-self. Stop spinning the same doubting thoughts in your head without action!
Turn your face towards the sun let the shadows fall behind you...

   Speaking of keep going.
Here I come with a small self-reflection to ease up the moment. These were some current doubting thoughts if continue travelling and bringing this book online shall be my thing. Trust me, to release this in writing, was not exactly easy. I wanted to do it for you and me. Do you feel it how we are moving forward together? ;O)
`Can I be a success if I refuse to be part of the social media, hash tagging, blogging, influencer ruled faking World? #dontlivefortheoutside #dowhatyoulike #bewhoyouare. Much aggressivity and negative connotation breeds from the way how too many people live only to show off without real value. Often, I'm being called an idealist - this is the nicest thing they say - but I believe that you will be up for us to meet halfway, if I state that everything human is better outside of the virtual World. We need real connections and physical experiences. As hard as it gets when facing reality with cold and hot and also some challenging and unpleasant dealings. Yet, it is what makes us people, people.

178

My life is not social media picture perfect. I don't want it to be this way. My life is real. It's a happy chaos. I might be an art deco. Geometrical, with some square, old-school habits, yet decorative. But my life and my style are my business to handle. I can learn to deal with any feelings and make it work for me. I am a totally everyday girl who, over time, grew a little more adventure than others. Just with a twist of curiosity. Just with a romantic mind to do well for others. Just with a naive idea that we are capable and can do anything. Just Sunshine with a little hurricane. I'm such a difficult person that I don't even understand myself. I sometimes want to give up and go and live on an uninhabited island and talk to my palm trees. The days when I face rudeness and rootless behaviour when my environment is inconsiderate and treats me like a piece of shit, those are the days when I feel like quitting. But what would I be quitting? What would I be quitting on? On the breaths I take. On the rising sun. On the water I drink. On the fresh healthy food, I eat to transform it into my amazing working body. On the wind caressing my skin. On the sea leaking my feet. On the beats my heart makes. On the people who love me, and I love them back. On the work which makes me feel matter and contributes to the better. On the moments when life fulfils. On all of that and much more. I like everything and like nothing at times. It can also be that I'm too simple and way to easy and feels good just by or with anything. Undoubtedly though, we need the dark to see the light. Without cold we won't feel the warmth. The sweetness tastes nothing when you haven't tried sour before. In our life everything must have an opposite pole for us to understand what it is. To describe and sense the real typicality of anything, you must recognise the opposite. The absence of such will not help. It will be useless and flat. It becomes indescribable and insignificant. It becomes nothing. So good and bad only exist side by side. We need them equally. It is my and your job to handle it properly, so it won't take up energy and the dark won't shorten the bright moments. It exists as a symbol as a shadow but have no impact on you. It becomes a measure to remind us of the goodness of the good. Why all this envy and showing up only the shiny sides when there is a lot out there. More than enough for everyone. Why wouldn't you smile or pass few good words to lift someone's day? It won't cost you anything and won't make you less well. I promise you in fact, it will make you be better and multiply your warmth and good vibe! Why would you not show interest in people and not cheer them when they do, create, say, sing, act, move, sport, give, draw, paint, walk, talk, dance, bake, cook, decorate, write something on their own. It is so great when one dares to express themselves and transparently shows all what they want to share to the World. You need a lot of courage to do that because we are all very vulnerable. You consider vulnerability as a weakness when it is the greatest strength one can have. It is the courage that makes you speak up and out loud when nobody left to stand up for you, it is the braveness what makes you fight for your goals when everyone else suggests you to resign from it; it is the push before you give up and quit your last strike, which makes you feel comfortable; it's like the last step before you cross the finish line of the marathon, just in a moment when you would collapse, but got you there. You have heard a thousand times and probably know for yourself that growth happens outside of your comfort zone. Here, I am, towing far out of mine. It's such a great place and a very tough one to live there for a longer time, but it is an opportunity which takes you long ahead and eventually, gives you your long-term dream. `

My father used to say: `it doesn't matter where you live but live good, you have got one short life`. It should not be taken too seriously. We can't waste time on feelings which are putting us down and making us quit on incredible and shaping challenges. Why would you choose the pain if you can grace and enjoy? When we are young, we believe that we have endless energy and we can do and go through anything. At a certain age, we start getting `serious`, we leave the restless kid's years behind and become an adult. As we age, our faith gets loose and we no longer see the plenty options around us. With my adventures, I wish to reassure you and everyone that the possibilities are there. They are yours forever of a lifetime. Don't lose the spark. Keep your young limitless spirit, keep going with open eyes, mind and heart. And take your grow-up experiences as your guard with you. On the journey, later, we will realise that life is short and getting shorter by the minute. With that realisation, we accept things easier, including our self. We take control over our mind and learn how to diss the unimportant. As our personality gets discovered, we care much less of others` judgement and opinions. That's freedom, for some it comes early for some late and for some it never comes. Try not to spend precious time, stressing over topics and matters which have no meaning and no impact on your life. It is better to light a candle than curse the darkness.

Easier said than done?

A belief repeated overtime becomes a fact. When practised a lot, everything becomes easy. That goes to problem-solving, finding comfort and relocation too!

Sometimes when I look at my friends, all settled with a cosy home, cushy job and sweet kids, I wish I would have stayed. But then I realize that it would not be me. My life could be different but, in this case, different wouldn't mean any better. And I say this as an exception. We all have an incomparable journey. If yours is to live cross-countries, I promise you, you will feel it when you set up for your first move.

But you must go away, so you can come back.

When I felt distressed, unsure and somehow lost – ready to throw in the towel and turn back – I looked for a familiar place. I looked at the sky. We all live under the same sky. We all look at the same sky. It is the same everywhere. It is home.

Drip-Drops

Less but more how.
Persistence makes the master!

`Titans are not the ones who never failed, they are the ones who have never stopped!` -Robin Sharma

Do not measure yourself to others, see if you have gotten better than yesterday.

Make the moments count.

Nothing is perfect and everything is as good as we value it.

You are capable of more than you know - Glinda to Oz

The secret of happiness is not found in seeking more, but in developing the capacity to enjoy less.

A belief repeated overtime becomes a fact. When practised a lot, everything becomes easy. That goes to problem-solving, finding comfort and relocation too!

A bird would never know if it can fly unless he jumps off the nest.

Just for fun

I love to do things just for fun. Like writing this little chapter for you, right here.
Enjoy!

I saw this scrappy rusty boat in the fishing village harbour today. Old car tires were hanged on the rims all around.

Is it for protection? For balance? For beauty? For attention?
You hang things around yourself too. All those things you buy, thinking that they make you happy, are weighing you down in reality. It is a moment of pleasure or a second of satisfaction, we are craving when life seems to be a long-stretched plateau of happenings. You and me and we all have a tendency to buy things when we crave some good feelings. You

can surely recall gloomy days when you went out on a hunt to purchase anything new. You scanned shops or looked at services to find any small or large possession you can get owned for yourself. That moment when you slammed the cash on the counter and you got hold of the thing, the same second the pleasure was gone.

Please take a moment to ask yourself:
What can you receive?
What you get is all a reflection of what you give!
Their love reflects yours; their kindness is a reflection of your kindness; their honesty is a reflection of your honesty and so on.
What's much and what's little? Relative! You measure in scope of your own experiences as that's your way to understand but when put on a different scale, bamm, you reconsider!
Do you know what makes life beautiful?
Everything and nothing.
Up to your senses! Depends what you see beautiful and what you allow yourself to notice!

   What do you enjoy?
When you have made your inventory, I give it a high chance that you have rather listed material things then experiences.
I enjoy the sound of the waives flipping the boats around and the ticking of the sail-poles when they hit each other in the wind. I feel the warmth of the sun on the 7th of January and it's the best to walk outside for hours, wearing only a light pullover. I sit on the warm stones and sunbathe like a lizard to collect all the heat and energy of the sun. Probably fell asleep

for few or more minutes and travelled on one of these funky colourful boats.

When you take time to soak in the moment, you start noticing that your senses are much more sensitive than you ever thought. It's not that it wasn't there before but you have been too busy or distracted to notice. Suddenly you see new colours. The clouds get shapes and forms and your imagination plays with them. The objects won't be what they physically are, but they take the shape and form of what your creativity makes up of them. The noises, sounds will surround you. You are included in every pitch and note of the movements and the stillness around you. Have you ever heard the shushing of the leaf and the quirking of the branches when you passed under a tree? It is very noisy out there even without a human word or sounds. I found nature or any environment, equally as tranquil as busy and expressive.

Then your smelling. You would be pretty sure to distinguish when passing a candy shop or McDonalds. They have a significant and very recognisable scent if you can call it a scent. It's a flavour which immediately waters your pallet and you feel it in your mouth. Not only such smells can be noticed, however. Smell of the fire or smoke, the dust, the fresh water, the leaf and the soil. Some experts can smell and taste thousand flavours, of course that needs long years of training. Yet, you can widen your own spectrum just by allowing your senses to notice a little bit more than in the everyday.

Stop looking for objects and material things and look out to feel. Joy will follow! Tame your senses and test them in many different settings. The sky is not the limit! Joy will come! I guarantee you!

There is a simpler option, not to be so mindful and sophisticated. You can enjoy activities, experiences and happenings rather than buying useless staff and accumulate them before you get them out of your house at the next spring-cleaning.
When you are a child you want everything immediately and you can't miss out on anything. You think that there is just now. And then later when you grow, you realise that there are things, you can't have, and you won't be able to do. So, you will selectively let go and pursue always less and less on a wide spectrum and more and more on a sharp focused path of your choice. That's how you start to know yourself and your call or as you call your lifestyle.
The most important thing is how you think about things. Because how you think, it forms your feelings and how you feel it shapes your life!
Be in control of your thoughts, choose them wise, choose them to serve your well-being. You will notice how your life changes a whole lot! Be at your best in your thoughts, so you live your best; whatever best means to you, in the actual moment or life-period.

What's a happy life?
You don't know and don't need to know!
Dream it up and make it yours.

Drip-Drops

Soak in the moment, make an imprint of its vibrations as life is too short to re-experience everything!

Be realistic: plan for a miracle.

"It's the possibility of having a dream come true that makes life interesting." — Paulo Coelho.

"The sunrise, of course, doesn't care
if we watch it or not.
It will keep on being beautiful
even if no one bothers to look at it."
Gene Amole

Bye for now and see you around

Life is a rollercoaster periods of fails and building new goals but what's important that you have your values and vision and you always stick to those. That makes your life easier and in all, in balance and gives you a safety feel.

I hope, I have spun your World around and spun you around the World a little. You might get the taste and start packing; or reconsidered and decided to settle where you are. Either way, I am happy that you took this journey and read along. I am grateful for spending this time together and wish you to carry some useful bits of the past pages.

When you have this sudden strike like `I'm experiencing this very odd feeling and it might be happiness! ` that's your sweet spot to remember how it happened.

What makes us different is our superpower! Go and conquer the World because the World won't be as wonderful without us in it!

Live the life you love and love the life you live!

Life is not happening to you; it is happening for you! Don't forget to dream and do more of what makes you happy.

Traditionally this goes in the Foreword, but I wanted to leave it as last to highlight it.

Dear Mom, Dad, deeply loved writing Buddy, Ags, Gesh, Harold, Petya, Yousef and my dearest Friends around the Globe. Thank you for believing in me. You had faith in me even after some procrastination and several detours in my writing. You still knew that I will make it. Even when momentarily I have lost my conviction.
You are amazing, and I dearly love you.

And thank you my reader for making it all the way till my last words. My greatest wish is that you feel just a little better, a little happier and a bit more certain on your next journey.

Happy Footloose!

About the Author

Marianna is a Globetrotter who has worked on various taskforce and implementation projects as a hospitality professional, living in eleven countries on three continents. She has revealed and developed her creativity and communication skills through her unorthodox methods of team training, coaching and consulting. Over the years, she has built a reputation as a person to lead any individual or team from tragic to magic. While on the footloose, she keeps sporting with various national target shooting and TRX groups. She is pleased to be one of the initiators to establish the first on-land coral nursery in the Seychelles.

Her past year was dedicated to stitch the snippets from her long-time notes and deduct her most significant learnings. She has summarized them in this book as a fun-packed collection for fellow adventure-desired hearts.

Made in the USA
Lexington, KY
16 December 2019